THE BEST OF
Birds&Blooms

Black-and-white
warbler, page 92

Table of Contents

ON THE FRONT COVER
*American goldfinch. Photo by
Agnieszka Bacal/Shutterstock*

ON THE TITLE PAGE
*Baltimore oriole. Photo by
Steve and Dave Maslowski*

Editorial

**ASSOCIATE
CREATIVE DIRECTOR**
Christina Spalatin

EXECUTIVE EDITOR
Kirsten Schrader

ART DIRECTOR
Kristen Stecklein

ASSOCIATE EDITOR
Julie Kuczynski

COPY CHIEF
Deb Warlaumont Mulvey

**PRODUCTION
COORDINATOR**
Jon Syverson

**SENIOR RIGHTS
ASSOCIATE**
Jill Godsey

Contributors

Lisa Ballard, Sheryl DeVore,
Kenn and Kimberly Kaufman,
Ken Keffer, Luke Miller,
Melinda Myers, Heather Ray,
Kelsey Roseth, Sally Roth,
David W. Shaw, Jill Staake

© 2020 RDA Enthusiast
Brands, LLC.
1610 N. 2nd St., Suite 102,
Milwaukee, WI 53212-3906

**International Standard
Book Number:**
D 978-1-61765-925-6
U 978-1-61765-926-3

Component Number:
D 118500055H
U 118500057H

**International Standard
Serial Number:** 1553-8400

Printed in USA
1 3 5 7 9 10 8 6 4 2

Pyrrhuloxia (left) and northern cardinal, page 106

Monarch butterfly, page 200

Welcome!

This fresh edition of *The Best of Birds & Blooms* is jam-packed with gorgeous photos, trusted expert advice and the most-loved stories from the past year.

Learn about backyard birds, get in-depth info on hummingbirds and discover new-to-you species.

You'll also find tips to attract birds and butterflies, as well as top-notch gardening pointers. A handy resource section offers feeding and growing basics.

We hope this book inspires you to connect with the beauty in your backyard and beyond.

—THE EDITORS OF
BIRDS & BLOOMS MAGAZINE

CHAPTER 1

Backyard Birds

Become familiar with the winged visitors right outside your window.

FROM LEFT: MARIE READ; JOHN GILL

BLACK-CAPPED CHICKADEE

Nature personality and scientist Laura Erickson posted on social media, "I think that I shall never see a poem as cute as a chickadee." From their cheery voice to their bold personalities, black-capped chickadees are undoubtedly adorable. Nearly identical, and equally cute, Carolina chickadees are found in the southeastern U.S. Enthusiastic eaters, chickadees can sometimes be coaxed to eat seeds right out of your hand.

One of the cutest birds, a black-capped chickadee, sits in a redbud tree.

Cutest of All

While beauty and charm are in the eye of the beholder, these chipper, pint-size birds will surely bring a smile to your face.

TUFTED TITMOUSE

It isn't the only crested bird around, but a tufted titmouse's peak certainly has the most flair. Both sexes always look styled and perfectly moussed, with vibrant black eyes to offset their pale expressive faces. With a range that's expanding northward, these birds are common feeder visitors in the East. They readily eat sunflower seeds, but it is especially amusing to watch them tackle whole peanuts in the shell.

A downy woodpecker stops for a snack at a peanut feeder.

DOWNY WOODPECKER

The daintiest of the woodpeckers, downies are familiar friends in backyards from coast to coast. They seem delicate even as they chisel out cavities in tree trunks, one chunk at a time. Downy woodpeckers eat a variety of foods, including seeds, fruits and insects, and they visit suet feeders throughout the year. No-melt suet is available for warmer months. But definitely serve high-fat treats during the winter months when downies need the extra nutrients.

NORTHERN CARDINAL

While male northern cardinals are stunningly bright and quite showy, females are no slouches in the cuteness category. They have subtle hints of blush that almost appear as if whimsically painted on. Cardinals prefer platform feeders for foraging on black oil sunflower and safflower feasts. If you don't have space for an additional feeder, add a tray to the bottom of your tube feeder to give cardinals a place to perch and eat.

RUBY-CROWNED KINGLET

Like feathered pingpong balls with toothpick legs, ruby-crowned kinglets bounce and flit about, flicking their wings in near constant motion. Kinglets are most visible in winter along the coasts and throughout the Southern states, but migrants show up anywhere. Despite their bug-filled diet, they occasionally nibble on suet cakes. Bold white eye-rings give these little nuggets personality. Red crown feathers are usually tucked away among the gray plumage.

Ruby-crowned kinglet in spruce tree

Male northern cardinal among crabapple tree blossoms

American goldfinch on flowering viburnum

AMERICAN GOLDFINCH

Goldfinches glow like beams of sunshine in summer and ebb to rich olive green in winter. These widespread cuties are recognized as the state bird of Iowa, New Jersey and Washington. While they eat a variety of seeds, a tube or sock feeder full of thistle is a magnet for finches. The fine seeds dry out if kept in storage for too long, so consider buying smaller bags rather than stocking up.

EASTERN BLUEBIRD

Along with their western counterparts, eastern bluebirds are beautifully patterned with rusty maroons that contrast against brilliant blues. Bluebirds perch conspicuously in open areas. To attract them, set out nesting boxes. You may even see some fledglings come summer! If you are lucky enough to have bluebirds in your neighborhood but not your yard, they might take mealworms from a feeder. Native landscapes with fruiting trees will also attract bluebirds to backyards.

An eastern bluebird turns its charming face toward the camera.

YELLOW WARBLER

Listen for the cheerful *sweet, sweet, sweet* tweets of yellow warblers in brushy habitats. You might see a lemon-hued male sporting orange streaks on his chest, or a soft yellow female. Warblers feed mostly on insects, so they generally aren't attracted to feeders. Instead, entice them to your garden by adding a water feature like a birdbath or, even better, a natural looking pond with flowing water.

It's the small size and intense eyes that make a northern saw-whet owl so captivating.

NORTHERN SAW-WHET OWL

Despite being named after the sound of sharpening blades on whetstones, the tiny northern saw-whet owl's charming calls are hardly menacing. The pint-size owls stand just about 8 inches tall, with oversized, endearing eyes. The alarm notes of songbirds may draw your attention to a roosting saw-whet owl in a dense conifer stand. You might also see the elusive birds at a banding program as researchers continue to learn more about their distribution, mostly in the forests of northern and western North America.

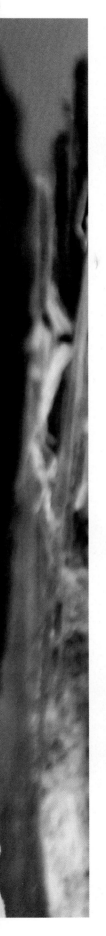

A dark-eyed junco shows off its cute pink bill.

DARK-EYED JUNCO

Juncos, called snowbirds across much of the continent, are harbingers of winter and holiday cheer, especially when traveling in flocks. For many years, separate types of juncos were classified as unique species, but now scientists identify them all as dark-eyed juncos. Most of them have delightful pink bills, and their white outer tail feathers flash as they fly by. These members of the sparrow family use brush piles for cover and feed on birdseed scattered directly on the ground.

HARD KNOCKS

You'd think repeatedly slamming their heads into hard surfaces would cause brain damage. Turns out woodpeckers have a special skull structure that protects their brains from the impact of pecking.

Yellow-bellied sapsucker

Get to Know Woodpeckers

A flash of ruby red or a proud scarlet crest peeking from behind a large tree limb signals that you've caught a glimpse of a woodpecker. With specialized skulls and quirky behaviors, the eight most common members of this intriguing family are anything but basic.

Red-headed
woodpecker

Yellow-Bellied Sapsucker

It's hard to see when they're foraging, but these sapsuckers do have hints of pale yellow on their stomachs. The size of a grosbeak, this bird is white and black with a red-peaked forehead and a short, sturdy beak; males also sport a red throat. Drilling holes in bark, they suck up the tree's sugary sap, hoping to snatch up insects. They are found throughout the eastern half of North America.

Red-Headed Woodpecker

Talk about a stunning species. This bold bird has a large, scarlet-colored head and spiky bill—and it's skilled at catching insects in midair. Both sexes sport a white belly, black back and white wing patches. Smaller than a crow, this Midwest and East Coast bird has a round, crestless head.

Downy Woodpecker

The downy woodpecker is the smallest and most common of this bunch, living year-round in most of the U.S. except the extreme Southwest. Slightly smaller than a robin, this cute bird has a pale belly, checkered black-and-white head and back, and, for a woodpecker, a bill that is surprisingly short. Males show a flash of red at the back of their heads.

Downy
woodpecker

HOST MORE
WOODPECKERS

Serve high fat peanuts
and suet or seeds to
attract woodpeckers.
Leave dead trees
standing in your yard,
provided they're safely
situated, to create
an insect buffet. Be
on the lookout for
woodpeckers like
red-headeds, Gilas or
downies caching food
in tree crevices. They
will retrieve it later for
winter sustenance.

Pileated
woodpeckers

TAILOR-MADE TONGUES

A woodpecker's long, barbed tongue makes retrieving insects a breeze. It extends far outside the bill and can be covered in a sticky fluid that helps capture bugs. Sapsuckers have an extra advantage: Hairlike structures on their short tongues help suck sticky, insect-laden sap from trees.

Gila woodpecker

Pileated Woodpecker

The pileated woodpecker is a behemoth and striking to behold. As soon as you spot one, you'll know. With a flaming red triangular crest, large size (nearly 20 inches!) and a wingspan close to 30 inches, this is the largest woodpecker in North America. Pileateds specialize in foraging for carpenter ants, drilling distinctive square holes into trees. They're found in Canada, the eastern U.S. and along the West Coast.

Red-Bellied Woodpecker

The name of this beautiful bird is misleading. Its belly is actually pale with tinges of red in the right light, and it has a black-and-white striped back with a bright red nape. Males also have a red crown. In the eastern U.S. where it lives, this bird can be seen picking at bark rather than drilling into it.

Gila Woodpecker

This noisy desert bird draws attention as it excavates tree trunks and saguaro cactuses for nesting cavities. Close to 10 inches long, Gilas are found in southern Arizona. They're sometimes spotted at hummingbird feeders, but Gilas primarily forage for fruit and insects, gleaning them from cactuses, trees and other plants.

Red-bellied woodpecker

Hairy woodpecker

Hairy Woodpecker

While its markings are similar to the downy's, the hairy woodpecker is about one-third larger, close to the size of a robin. Its chisel-shaped bill is prominent, about the same length as its head. Its coloring varies across North America, and at times it appears to be stained with brown watercolors and has less spotting.

Northern Flicker

With markings unlike those of any others on this list, northern flickers have a black bib, spotted belly, white rump and a brownish gray back patterned with spots, bars and crescents. Males also may show red or black whiskers, a red nape crescent and stripes of yellow or red throughout their tail feathers. Larger than a blue jay and found across North America, this bird often forages on the ground.

Northern
flicker

Meet the Jays

A look at the bold, sassy birds that liven up the feeder scene across America.

STELLER'S JAYS, like blue jays and some others, occasionally stir things up by imitating the voices of hawks.

BLUE JAYS, among the most familiar fliers in the Corvid family, live year-round in the eastern U.S. and parts of southern Canada.

WESTERN SCRUB-JAYS were split into two species in 2016: the Woodhouse's and the California. This striking bird is a California scrub-jay.

CLEVER AND BRAZEN, jays belong to the brainy Corvid family. Each species has its own personality and habits, and all except the Canada jay are gardeners: They cache seeds and nuts by shoving them into the soil to retrieve later. Uneaten caches sprout into new oaks, walnuts, pines and other trees to keep forests renewed...or to tickle us with an unexpected cluster of sunflower seedlings.

Nearly all jays are blue, and most are about the size of a robin. But here's a surprise for those who only know blue jays—most species lack a crest. Only blue and Steller's jays sport a pointy tuft of head feathers; the others look more like overgrown bluebirds. They're all year-round birds, so stock that feeder, fill the birdbath and get ready to be entertained by their antics!

Steller's Jay

These dark, elegant, long-crested jays are named for Georg Steller, naturalist on the 1741 expedition of Captain Bering, not for their stellar looks (notice the spellings). Their range takes over where the blue jay's leaves off, from the Rockies to the Pacific. Birds of the interior have white face markings; coastal birds, blue face streaks. Common at feeders and in coniferous forests, Steller's jays frequent campgrounds and state and national parks, tempting visitors to ignore the "do not feed wildlife" signs.

Blue Jay

When a jay screams to signal danger, other birds instantly flee, which can save their lives. Everything about these big, boisterous birds says, "Notice me!" Unless they don't want to be seen, that is. Like all

MEXICAN JAYS reside in groups year-round in mountain areas near the border.

ONE MENU FOR MOST

Sunflower seeds, whole corn kernels and peanuts, in or out of the shell, in a tray feeder invite all but Canada jays. Add a block of suet, which every species eats. Then have fun experimenting with these omnivores! Try dog kibble, peanut butter or even food scraps to see what your jays like best.

jays, even loudmouth blue jays are super sneaky around the nest. Blue jays are the only migratory jays in North America, but you'll still see them year-round; not all migrate, and others move in when migrants leave. Common across the eastern two-thirds of the continent, they're expanding westward.

Western Scrub-Jay

Now split into two nearly look-alike species, the California scrub-jay of coastal regions and Woodhouse's scrub-jay of the interior, these bold blue-and-gray jays are common across lower elevations of the West, where they frequent shrubby areas and backyards. Both make scolding cries and sing sweet, quiet, musical songs when with their mates, as most jay species do. A close relative, the island scrub-jay, lives only on California's Santa Cruz Island.

Florida Scrub-Jay

Housing development has been tough on this federally recognized endangered species as its scrub oak homelands slowly disappear or are carved into ever smaller pieces. Acorns are Florida scrub-jays' main food—a single bird may cache 6,000 or more each year. Feeders stocked with peanuts help sustain them.

Mexican Jay

At first, all crestless blue-colored jays seem to look similar. This species is known for its bicolor markings—blue above and gray below—and nasal *wink?* calls. Found in the mountains of Arizona, New Mexico and Texas, Mexican jays stay in groups even at nesting time, when they share feeding duty for hungry nestlings.

GREEN JAYS are the most colorful Corvids. Spotting one requires a trip to the southernmost part of Texas.

CANADA JAYS rarely stray from home base, northern evergreen forests, but they do follow hikers or stop by picnic or campsites, begging for leftover food.

PINYON JAYS stuff their esophagi with up to 40 pinyon pine seeds, stashing them away to eat later.

Green Jay

A highlight of the birding hot spot of Brownsville, Texas, this tropical jay is expanding its range, with sightings all the way to Laredo, Corpus Christi and even San Antonio, almost 300 miles north. Look for green jays at feeders at state parks and refuges, where they enjoy oranges and grape jelly, but also peanuts, sunflower seeds and corn. Water is a big attraction, too.

Canada Jay

Endearingly tame and undeniably cute, these jays, formerly known as gray jays, don't look or act like other jays! Fluffy gray and white, with a small bill suited to twisting off meat, Canada jays live in boreal, coniferous forests of the far North and high in the western mountains. So tame that they will eat right from a human hand, these jays are famed for approaching hikers, hunters and campers. Meat is what they want, or bread, suet and other soft foods, which they cache in bark or branches, not in the soil. Nuts and seeds at feeders are less appealing to them. These calm jays tend to be more silent than their kin. It's other nesting birds that sound the alarm when one comes near, because nestlings are just more meat to a Canada jay.

Pinyon Jay

This western species is in dramatic decline—down by an estimated 85% since 1970. Much of its tree and shrubby habitat has been turned into grazing lands. These short-tailed jays roam in big flocks to find meaty pinyon pine nuts, uttering nasal *caws* to keep in touch. Look for them from Montana to Oregon, south to New Mexico and Arizona. P.S. No need to break the bank buying pine nuts: They'll eat the usual jay menu of sunflower seeds, peanuts, corn and suet.

LISTEN FOR THE WHISTLE

Because Baltimore orioles feed high in trees, their rich, varied whistles and chattering calls are often heard before the birds are spotted in the canopies.

Blaze Orange

Tempt colorful nectar-loving Baltimore orioles with sugar water and ripe fruit.

GENE STRATTON-PORTER, a naturalist in the early years of the 20th century, described the Baltimore oriole as "spilling notes of molten sweetness, as it shot like a ray of detached sunshine." It's true, nothing brightens a day like this member of the blackbird family, thanks to its striking orange breast, black head and white-barred wings, plus its bold, melodic call.

Baltimore orioles are one of eight orioles found in North America. Its relatives are Bullock's, orchard, spot-breasted, hooded, Audubon's, Scott's and Altamira. Where the ranges of Bullock's and Baltimore overlap in the Midwest, the two sometimes interbreed.

About 8 inches long, with a 9- to 12-inch wingspan, Baltimores are medium-sized songbirds. Like all other blackbirds, they have a thick, pointed bill. The male's vibrant underparts, shoulders and rump can vary from flaming orange to yellow-orange. Mature females and juveniles tend to be more dull, with yellow-brown feathers and dark barred wings.

These flamboyant birds spend winters from the southeastern states through Central America and northern South America. They migrate north from Georgia to southern Canada to breed. In early spring and summer, they may hang around your yard if they like the sugar water in your oriole or hummingbird feeders. Halved oranges, grape jelly, red cherries and red grapes also attract them, but not yellow cherries or green grapes. Baltimore orioles dine on ripe, dark-colored fruit, nectar and insects, which they sometimes catch in the air. They'll also hang upside down or perform other quite athletic moves to catch bugs or caterpillars.

During the spring mating season, males attract females by singing, chattering and hopping from branch to branch. If a female is interested, the male bows and fans his wings and tail, then the female responds by singing and quivering her wings.

After pairing, the female weaves a pouch-shaped nest that hangs from the end of a deciduous tree branch, usually on the edge of an airy woodland. Elms, cottonwoods, maples, willows and apple trees are among their favored nesting sites. The female lays three to six pale gray-blue eggs, which take two weeks to hatch. Both parents care for the chicks, which fledge two weeks later.

If there's no threat of raptors or cats, a mother oriole may bring her fledglings to a backyard feeder. In addition to fruit and sugar water, you can lure Baltimore orioles to your yard with nectar-producing tubular flowers and native trees and shrubs that bear dark-colored fruit. Then listen each spring for their loud, rich song in a tree above you, as if they're whistling a tune to tell you where to find them.

EASY TO PLEASE
An orange half on a flat surface keeps an oriole happy. Feeders for oranges are available but not necessary.

"I love Baltimore orioles' colors and gorgeous song. When they sing, it's like happiness put to birdsong."

Grace Huffman
OKLAHOMA CITY, OKLAHOMA

CATERPILLAR CONNOISSEUR
These flashy fliers dine on furry caterpillars that other birds won't touch. They whack them on a branch to remove the hair, then gulp them down.

SQUIRT!
Baltimore orioles use a technique called gaping to get juice out of fruit. They stab a ripe berry with a closed bill, then open wide and lap up the droplets with their tongues.

The Golden Birds

Bring bright, thistle-loving beauties to your backyard.

SEEING A VIBRANT YELLOW American goldfinch at a feeder is enough to make any birder's heart skip a beat. Among the muted plumage of pine siskins, chickadees and sparrows, these bright beauties are a shock to the system.

"They are very striking," says Scott Gremel, a wildlife biologist at Washington's Olympic National Park. "They look like tropical birds."

Male and female goldfinches appear markedly different during breeding season, when males molt into bright yellow body feathers with black wings and cap and an orange bill. Juveniles and females are less colorful year-round. In winter, males have a dark bill and dull yellow body feathers, and look more like the females.

These feathered friends mainly eat seeds, cracking them open with their short bills. Favorite seeds include Njyer, thistle, black oil sunflower, alder and aster, among others. They also snack on buds, sap, the bark of young twigs, and occasionally insects.

To attract them to your yard, plant native thistles or milkweed. While they eat from the ground, they're adapted to pluck seeds from swaying flower heads and feeders.

Use tube feeders with short perches to encourage goldfinches and to discourage sparrows. Sock feeders also dispense tiny thistle seeds and are attractive to finches, pine siskins and chickadees.

American goldfinches' breeding range includes southern Canada all the way to northern Georgia and coastal California. In winter, they vacate the northern edge of this range, and flocks appear south to Florida and the Mexican border.

Goldfinches aren't under threat. Partners in Flight, a conservation organization, estimates a breeding population of 42 million. Found in cities and agricultural areas, "they are a species that has done well with human settlement," Scott says.

These active birds have bouncy, aerobatic flight patterns. They pair off during breeding season, but other times of the year, they may fly in flocks of 50 to 100. "If you see a weedy field full of thistle, sometimes there will be a huge flock of goldfinches," Scott says.

The in-flight call of the goldfinch sounds like *po-ta-to-chip*. Its other songs and calls are random series of warbles and twitters that last a few seconds, while its courtship call is a sharp *tee-yee* with a burst of song.

After couples pair up and select a nest site in a bush or shrub—not too high off the ground—females build an open cup nest. It's woven with plant fibers and rootlets. It's supported by spider silk, and the inside is lined with fluffy material taken from seed heads.

Most fledglings leave the nest 11 to 17 days after hatching, so by late summer you may see olive-colored youngsters at your feeders.

Goldfinches, like this female, perch on zinnias to eat the flowers' seeds.

HUGELY POPULAR

The American goldfinch is so widespread and beloved, it's the state bird of three states. You may hear people refer to these sunny finches as eastern or willow goldfinches, depending on where you are in the U.S.

"We never had goldfinches visit until my family put out a thistle feeder. We had a pair within three hours. I love the pop of color they bring to my yard!"

Jessica Paoletti
NEW CASTLE, DELAWARE

MULTIPLE MATES

A female typically selects one partner, though afterward she sometimes mates with another male.

FAVORITE FLOWERS

Goldfinches are especially drawn to the seeds of sunflowers, coneflowers, asters and grasses.

LATE BLOOMER

Goldfinches wait to breed until June or July, when milkweed and thistle seeds are plentiful. The birds use the seeds to build nests and feed their young.

HOLDING ON
Thanks to a large, backward-facing claw on each foot, red-breasted nuthatches grip tree bark and traverse up and down trunks.

Tiny Acrobats

Serve sunflower seeds and suet to welcome nimble red-breasted nuthatches.

Brown-headed nuthatch

BLARING SHARP, tin-hornlike calls no matter the weather, busy red-breasted nuthatches add life to even the chilliest days. Frequent visitors at feeders, the incredibly active 4½-inch-long birds are quite at home there, snatching suet, peanuts, mealworms and other goodies with their thin bills.

Male red-breasted nuthatches boast a rusty breast, blue-gray wings, black cap, white eyebrow, black eye line and white throat. Females have a lighter red breast and gray cap.

Adept climbers, they glide up and down trunks and branches in search of beetles, spiders, ants and other insects in warm months.

The birds seem almost tame, as they're more intent on eating than reacting to your presence. That offers the opportunity to observe their interesting behaviors, says Nancy Castillo, author of the *Zen Birdfeeder* blog and owner of a Wild Birds Unlimited shop in Saratoga Springs, New York.

"Watch them take a seed or nut from the feeder, fly to a nearby tree, and tuck it away in the bark crevices," Nancy says. "They may then hack away at it to open it or leave it for retrieval later." To survive in winter when insects are difficult to find, the intelligent birds remember where they stored seeds and larvae to reclaim when they need them.

Red-breasted nuthatches live year-round in coniferous forests across southern Canada and the northern United States. Their range also includes mountainous regions of the Southwest and the eastern U.S. In fall, these birds fly south—sometimes reaching the Gulf Coast in September or October—searching for food.

Every two or three years, their movement brings more nuthatches than usual, in a large migration called an irruption.

Nuthatches are expanding their breeding range in some eastern states where habitats are suitable. Come spring, they fly north to breed within coniferous spruce, fir and hemlock forests or mixed forests that include aspens.

To attract a female, the male sings a melody that's drastically different from its typical harsh call. He droops his wings, raises his head and sways back and forth. Pairs might also fly side by side in long, exaggerated gliding patterns.

The female does most of the hard work for nesting, excavating a cavity in a dead or partially alive aspen, birch or conifer, sometimes using a natural opening. She builds a nest of moss, fur, feathers, pine needles and other materials, then lays five to eight white eggs with reddish brown spots. They hatch in about 12 days, and both parents feed their young until the fledglings leave the nest 18 to 21 days later.

FOUR OF A KIND
Red-breasted, pygmy, white-breasted and brown-headed nuthatches live in North America. Their names offer helpful hints for identification.

WHAT'S IN A NAME?
The word *nuthatch* likely comes from a Middle English phrase meaning "nut hacker."

"Red-breasted nuthatches like eating straight from my garden! I plant sunflowers for them, since they enjoy the seeds."
Sue Gronholz
BEAVER DAM, WISCONSIN

STICKY TRICKS
Uniquely skilled and crafty, red-breasted nuthatches use flakes of bark to smear sticky pine and spruce resin at nest hole entrances, a tactic that may deter predators.

Northern Nomads

The resilient common redpoll brings lively cheer to cool-weather feeders.

IMAGINE A SONGBIRD as hardy as a polar bear but as tiny as a pine siskin. The common redpoll is that bird. A member of the finch family, this tough little creature thrives in the harshest and coldest environments.

The farther south you are, the less likely you are to see a redpoll. Even in the north, they move in unpredictable ways within their range, following food sources. A flock might clean out a feeder in a day during some winters...or it might not show up at all.

"Common redpolls stay in the northern latitudes if food is readily available," explains Emma Greig, a program leader for Project FeederWatch, which is organized by the Cornell Lab of Ornithology. "They're fun to watch because they constantly sort out dominance."

These hungry birds usually snack on small seeds from grasses and trees, plus catkins and buds in spring and insects in summer. Groups fly in big acrobatic flocks. Alighting for a moment on one branch and then flitting to another, the petite backyard visitors are in constant motion and continually displace each other at feeders. Ones that can't manage to push their way through the crowd eat from the ground.

Emma recommends Nyjer seeds for attracting redpolls because the seeds are so small and oily. "Cold weather birds appreciate the fat," she says. They like sunflower and millet seeds, too.

These sturdy birds breed near the Arctic Circle, where they stay in willow and alder thickets, the edges of birch and spruce forests and bushy areas on the tundra. When it comes time to attract a mate, the male flies in circles while he sings and offers food.

Once paired, the female builds her nest of twigs, grass and moss on a low branch, then lines it with grouse feathers or fur. If she calls the tundra home, her nest might rest on rock ledges or shrubby ground covers. Mother redpolls lay four to seven green eggs with purple spots, which hatch in about 10 days. Chicks grow quickly, fledging after only 12 days.

Adults are about 5 inches long, with white bars on each wing and a red patch on their foreheads. They also have dark legs, yellow beaks, white bellies and notched tails. Males sport a reddish wash on their chests. There are two kinds of redpolls but the paler one, the hoary redpoll, stays in the Arctic, rarely visiting feeders in Canada.

It's easy to confuse redpolls with other brown finches, like house finches, which also have red on their heads and chests. To verify whether you're seeing a redpoll, look for the black patch around its bill and listen for its whistle-like *zap!* and *dreeee!*

SAVING IT FOR LATER
Redpolls stash seeds for several hours in a pouch in their throats. That useful sac stores up to 2 grams of food, or about a quarter of the birds' daily energy requirement.

"Some years redpolls are prevalent at feeders, and some years they are uncommon. Their movements show us what's happening with native, wild foods."

Emma Greig
PROGRAM LEADER,
PROJECT FEEDERWATCH

SNOWBIRDS
Some birds take shelter in birdhouses or tree cavities when it gets cold outside, but not redpolls. These chill-resistant fliers sometimes roost under the snow to insulate themselves from subzero temperatures.

TINY BIRD, BIG APPETITE

Redpolls eat the equivalent of about a third of their body weight every day. To attract them, plant a birch tree. In some areas, redpolls subsist mostly on birch seed.

Hooo's Hiding in Your Backyard

More often heard than seen, these 10 elusive owls may be among your neighborhood regulars.

A northern pygmy-owl peeks its head out of a tree cavity, which was most likely created naturally or by a woodpecker.

The feathers of this gray morph eastern screech-owl offer natural camouflage.

Great horned owls lay eggs in winter, and protect their nestlings until they are ready to leave the nest in late spring.

SECRECY AND STEALTH, plus the cover of darkness, keep most owls out of view. Seeing one is so special, you might think these raptors are rare birds. But they're actually all around you, hidden in plain sight.

To avoid discovery, owls perch motionless, nearly invisible in their superb camouflage. Still, other birds sometimes spot them and immediately raise a ruckus—so when you hear that kind of commotion, take a look.

And tune in at night, when most species are hootin' and hollerin', each with its own unique voice. Once you start listening for owls, you'll discover they're not rare birds at all—but definitely remarkable!

Great Horned Owl

The deep hoots of these big birds (with a wingspan of 4½ feet!) are heard at night across North America in every habitat, even in cities. They're most vocal in winter, so bundle up and step outside for a listen. Their favorite food? Skunks! But their full menu is a long one, including crows and other birds, frogs, shrews, bats, rabbits and other small mammals.

A barred owl rarely strays more than a few miles from its nest cavity. Below: Look for a square-shaped head and dark bill when identifying western screech-owls.

Barred Owl

Known for its call, *Who cooks for you? Who cooks for you all?*, this common, noisy species of the East, Midwest and Northwest is mostly nocturnal. Unlike many of its relatives with yellow eyes, the barred owl has dark eyes, which enhance its mysterious appearance.

Screech-Owl

Worms, moths, mice, birds and other tidbits go down the hatch of these small owls. About the size of a beer glass, the look-alike eastern and western species are usually gray, but some eastern birds are rusty red and some westerners are brown. Their voices are the giveaway; the eastern lets loose with an unearthly trilled whinny, while the western has a bouncing ball call that starts slow and picks up speed.

A DRINK IN THE DARK

Screech-owls are fond of water, so get in the habit of looking for one at your birdbath or water feature at night. You won't hear the bird arrive because an owl's feathers are specially made for silence—the super soft surface and fringed edges keep prey (and us) from hearing them swoop in.

Long-eared owls are secretive and quiet, but they sometimes roost in dense evergreen trees.

Identify short-eared owls by their pale, round faces and buff wing patches.

Long-Eared Owl

When roosting, this uncommon owl stretches itself tall and thin, extending upward and flattening its feathers to disguise its shape. Not a backyard bird, it roosts in dense cover near open land where it hunts at night for mice, birds and other prey. Its range covers most of the U.S., but at different seasons. Listen for long hoots or barking.

Short-Eared Owl

Look twice at the next northern harrier you see gliding over a meadow or marsh, especially in the early morning or late afternoon, it may be the short-eared owl, a daytime hunter in wide-open spaces. Fall through early spring is its prime time, as its winter range covers the entire country.

Northern Saw-Whet Owl

That's whet, like whetstone, not wheat. This robin-sized owl's call sounds like the repeated rhythm of sharpening a saw. A rodent eater, this nocturnal owl is famously tame. In fall, saw-whets spread out from their breeding grounds in northern states and western mountains, wintering in thickets and woods across the country.

Northern saw-whet owls are so small, they often eat an adult mouse over the course of two meals.

Snowy owl

Snowy Owl

A winter report of a snowy owl in the Lower 48, usually at a beach, airport or field, draws bird lovers from miles around to see the elegant visitor from the Arctic. The huge bird sits nearly motionless for hours between daytime hunting forays for rabbits, rodents, geese, herons or other birds. Lemmings are its mainstay up north in the tundra.

Burrowing Owl

When you see a prairie dog colony, take a closer look at those little upright figures—because burrowing owls may be among them! These small owls don't eat the animals whose burrows they move into; instead, they share watchdog duties. Beetles are a favorite prey, along with other insects, lizards, birds and mice. Birds of the West, some migrate down to Mexico and even farther south in winter. A subspecies that digs its own burrows lives year-round in Florida.

Barn Owl

If you've ever seen a big, ghostly bird swoop through the beam of headlights, you probably glimpsed a barn owl. They often patrol roadsides as well as towns, cities and wild lands for rodents. You won't hear this one hooting; instead, hissing screams are its signature call. It's widespread across all but the far northern tier of states.

Northern Pygmy-Owl

It's advantageous that the pygmy-owl is so tiny—this daytime hunter is one of the fiercest birds in North America, snatching up chickadees, kinglets and even hummingbirds! Only a slight bit bigger than a house sparrow, the northern pygmy-owl lives in the forests of the western mountains, where it repeatedly toots during the day.

Burrowing owls look for food day and night, taking naps by their burrow entrances in between hunts.

A heart-shaped white face is a characteristic that sets the barn owl apart from other species.

HOME, SWEET HOME

Screech, barred, great horned and barn owls are common nighttime birds in yards across the country, often scouting feeder areas for rabbits, skunks, mice and other such critters that come out at night to nibble spilled seed. Convince them to stay with nest boxes; all except the great horned readily take to them. Put up the box in late fall, as courtship and nesting begin in winter.

Berry Lovers

As insects disappear, trees and shrubs produce persistent bite-sized fruits. Watch these winter residents dine on the cold-season feast.

Bohemian waxwing on mountain ash tree

American robin
in a berry-filled
hawthorn

EATING SOCIALLY

In winter, when varied thrushes forage for berries and nuts, they form loose flocks around favorite fruit producers, including apple and dogwood trees, and blueberry and thimbleberry plants.

Varied thrush on viburnum

An eastern bluebird perches among snow-covered winterberries.

Thrushes

Robins and bluebirds are the thrushes you usually see in winter. But the varied thrush of the Northwest, the Townsend's solitaire of the West, and the widespread hermit thrush also stay all winter. Hermit and varied thrushes feed on a variety of berries, often alone. Solitaires live up to their name in winter, each fiercely guarding its own chosen trees from berry-eating relatives. They gobble the juniper berries as well as those of the mistletoe that grows on the trees. In a scanty year for juniper berries, the high-fat mistletoe makes up the difference in solitaires' diets.

Bluebirds

After insects dwindle, bluebirds heavily depend on berries, and small wintering groups are always on the lookout. Winterberry is practically guaranteed to bring in nearby bluebirds, but its bright red berries disappear fast once the birds spot them. Evergreen holly, hawthorn and native junipers like eastern red cedar provide a much bigger banquet, attracting bluebirds for several weeks. Almost any type of berry is fair game, including those of poison ivy. In late winter, look for bluebirds at the fuzzy spires of staghorn sumac, along with birds like robins, northern flickers and downy woodpeckers.

INSTANT APPEAL

Young plants such as native junipers, bayberry and myrtles, and tree-type evergreen hollies take years to bear fruit. The eventual berry buffet is worth the wait, though. Just be patient, fertilize properly and irrigate infrequently. For a faster payoff, go for winterberry or arrowwood shrubs, and ornamental crabapple or hawthorn trees. Choose mature shrubs and trees, and you'll see winter birds enjoying them the very first year.

Yellow-rumped
warbler on
bayberry branch

Yellow-Rumped Warblers

The wood warbler that winters most widely in North America owes its success to myrtle berries (*Myrtus*), including bayberry and other natives. Unlike nearly every other bird that eats the berries—bluebirds, thrushes, robins, waxwings, flickers and more—yellow-rumps, once called myrtle warblers, are able to digest the waxy coating, transforming it into fat that helps them survive the cold. They also eat the berries of juniper, poison ivy, poison oak and Virginia creeper. If you're near a bayberry or other myrtle, listen for a signature sharp *chip*. Tree swallows, the only other birds capable of turning myrtle wax into vital fat, join the warblers at myrtles in their coastal wintering areas.

Cedar Waxwings

A juniper tree (*Juniperus virginiana*) is responsible for the common name of cedar waxwings, which flock to the blue-gray fruit in winter. "Flocking" is the word, because these social birds do nearly everything as a group. They have no home territory except at nesting time. Berries are the bulk of their diet year-round, and finding food motivates their movements. Look for wandering winter waxwings at flowering crab, hawthorn, mountain ash, deciduous or evergreen hollies, junipers, toyon and more—any berry producer that offers a feast big enough for a flock.

A small flock of cedar waxwings gathers on a crabapple tree.

KEEPING IT BALANCED

About a quarter of a downy woodpecker's diet consists of plant materials like berries, acorns and grains. The rest is made up of larvae and other bugs.

Downy woodpecker on American bittersweet

Northern
mockingbird
calling from an
icy hawthorn tree

Woodpeckers

One at a time is the general rule for woodpeckers at winter berries. Even though they're mostly singletons, what a variety you may see! Every woodpecker, flicker and sapsucker that's around in winter seeks out berries, especially poison oak and poison ivy. These are a problem for humans, but to birds, they're a prize. Just like other berry eaters, woodpeckers "plant" seeds of the berries they eat via their droppings, which can sprout into a welcome bonus—or extra weeding duty.

Northern Mockingbirds

An entertaining bully, this big, bold bird is a loner in winter. Expect occasional skirmishes at the berries, because mockingbirds are notoriously territorial. Bittersweet, viburnums, crabapples, hawthorns, hollies, pyracantha, roses with small

hips (including the invasive multiflora) and a long list of other berries go down the hatch. A wintering brown thrasher or gray catbird may also be drawn to the same berries, but these mockingbird relatives have much better manners.

American Robins

Robins have something of a seasonal split personality—in summer, they're backyard birds, hopping about the lawn; in winter, they retreat to woods' edges and stay in flocks. In recent years, some individuals have begun to buck the usual trend and become feeder regulars. Look for a single backyard robin, or an entire roaming flock, at hawthorn, holly, juniper, pyracantha, hackberry, beautyberry, arrowwood and viburnum, toyon, sumac, and other plants with persistent berries that hang on branches through winter.

CHAPTER 2

Amazing Hummingbirds

Delight in the beauty of these fliers and learn easy ways to attract them to your yard.

Flying Jewels

It takes a lot of patience, a bit of skill and some luck to capture a winning photo of these tiny, fast-flying birds. *Birds & Blooms* readers rose to the challenge in the magazine's first hummingbird photo contest. Here are the stories behind some of the best shots.

WINNER
HUMMINGBIRD
PHOTO CONTEST

I am a self-taught amateur photographer, and my favorite subject is hummingbirds. Every year I grow hummingbird-friendly plants near my back porch. What makes photographing the fliers a challenge is I have a C4 injury and am quadriplegic, with full use of only one arm. I used my manufacturing engineering degree to design a mount for my wheelchair that helps me hold the camera. I press the shutter button using a corded release with my tongue, which takes the picture. In this photo it appears the ruby-throated hummingbird has transparent wings; I like to keep a little blur for extra motion.

Mike Bond
SUMTER, SOUTH CAROLINA

A rufous hummingbird bathed and preened in my backyard fountain. The rufous is sometimes hard to differentiate from the Allen's hummingbird, but with all the rust coloring and the notched tail feather, there was no doubt of its identity.

Catherine Werth
RAMONA, CALIFORNIA

An Anna's hummingbird graced me with a nest in my front yard. I watched the entire fascinating process up close. This shot was taken a few days before the hatchling fledged. The momma bird was just about to feed her baby. She was a very attentive mother.

Anne Winder-Steed
SAN DIEGO, CALIFORNIA

This female ruby-throat seemed to enjoy a summer day from her elevated roost in my yard. She is perched on a kousa dogwood tree fruit. To give you an idea of just how small she is, note that the fruit is just 2 to 3 centimeters in diameter. Her petite body isn't even bending the stem! It truly gives a sense of the hummingbird's diminutive size.

Lucinda Moriarty
EAST HAMPTON,
CONNECTICUT

For a few weeks during migration I am lucky to have rufous hummingbirds visit my garden. This female stopped to put on a show, flaring her tail feathers aggressively. Their stays are short, but they defend their territory fiercely, hassling all the other hummingbirds.

Dalya Hansen
REDDING, CALIFORNIA

A ruby-throat was drinking my homemade nectar (no red dye here!) from a red glass feeder in May. I believe it may be one of a pair from the previous year, as it knew exactly where the feeder was.

Stacie York
LITTLE MEADOWS, PENNSYLVANIA

Every September hummingbirds gather in the dozens at Longfellow Gardens, located in Minneapolis, Minnesota, before they head south for winter. I captured this shot of a ruby-throat with my Nikon D750. The bird was taking a quick break before zipping off to sip from another flower.

Justin Pruden
ST. PAUL, MINNESOTA

While visiting Texas Hill Country, my wife, Kathe, and I went for a hike on a friend's land. Kathe spotted this wonderfully camouflaged black-chinned hummingbird nest. We watched the female feed her young while the male briefly buzzed around the nest. It was such a neat scene that I decided to return the very next day and set up a blind.

I didn't want to simply take a typical close-up photo. Instead I positioned my camera, a Canon EOS-1D with a 500 mm lens, so that I could catch the male if he performed the same behavior. I had to wait only three or four hours. I have photographed many hummingbirds, but this is my favorite shot.

John Hendrickson
CLIPPER MILLS, CALIFORNIA

While at Wild Outdoor World of Arizona, I used a Canon EOS to capture this male Anna's. Hummingbirds come and go constantly at the preserve, located near Tucson and open by appointment. After sipping a bit of nectar, this Anna's returned to his favorite perch, and when he landed, the sun began to shine. The hummingbirds at Wild Outdoor World are in their natural habitat and accustomed to people.

Tom Mast
LUTZ, FLORIDA

This female ruby-throat holds a special place in my heart. My husband and I saved her from certain death after she got trapped in the upper rafters of our garage. The photo was taken in fall, just one day before she migrated south. I like to think she treated me to a photo session in gratitude for saving her life.

Kerry Loving
CARLISLE, IOWA

The colors of this male Anna's coordinated perfectly with the red-flowering currant plant he visited.

Leslie Scopes Anderson
ARCATA, CALIFORNIA

Painted lady butterflies were migrating at the same time as hummingbirds, and my flowers were covered in both! This ruby-throat gave up chasing the butterflies away and decided to share.

Linda Petersen TERRIL, IOWA

I was photographing butterflies at Grant Park in South Milwaukee, Wisconsin, when this ruby-throat flew in to collect nectar from a helianthus bloom.

Todd Leech SOUTH MILWAUKEE, WISCONSIN

As the sun sets, my favorite thing to do is watch my hummingbirds get their fill of sweetness before nightfall. I took this photo one summer evening on my deck with a Nikon D7100.

Lisa Hostetter
WAVERLY, MISSOURI

Kimberly and Kenn Kaufman found this nest in their yard.

A Marvel in Miniature

A dream of finding an active hummingbird nest came true.

IN THE EAST, there's one breeding hummingbird species, but it's a good one! Ruby-throated hummingbirds are real charmers. The tiny birds have so much attitude and charisma that it definitely makes up for the lack of hummingbird diversity in our region.

When my husband, Kenn, and I got married and moved into our first home, it didn't seem likely that there would be many birds nesting in our yard, let alone a hummer. The house was in the country, but it was surrounded on all sides by the monoculture of farm fields: mostly corn, wheat and soybeans. Our landscape had a few mature trees, including maples and pines, but not much else to entice a discerning bird looking for a place to raise its young. But we hung our feeders and hoped.

Top: A female ruby-throated hummingbird tends to her thimble-sized nest. Bottom: Young ruby-throats, like these two, stay in the nest for about three weeks before fledging.

Hummingbirds found our feeders, and we were thrilled. But to be honest, we never even thought of looking for a nest. Then one afternoon while we were in the backyard, a hummer buzzed by and flew into one of the pines. We stood in utter astonishment as she began to work on what appeared to be the makings of a nest! Kenn dashed for the scope, and we spent the next four hours watching this industrious little fairy as she labored to create her haven.

What female hummingbirds lack in size they make up for in productivity. Males do not take part in nesting, so females do the work building the nest, incubating the eggs and raising the young.

And speaking of the tiny nest, what an amazing example of miniature architecture! From the day we discovered "our" female beginning to build the nest, it took six days for her to finish the mini masterpiece. The list of building materials sounds more like a spell from a Harry Potter book than nest material. Spiderwebs and plant down are covered with carefully selected lichens, stuck to the nest exterior to help camouflage both the structure and the young.

After watching for many hours, I finally surrendered to the call of duty and went inside to get some work done. Half an hour later, Kenn came rushing into the house with a dazed look on his face, saying, "You've got to come out here and see this."

Outside—in the front yard this time—was another nest! Less than 30 yards from the one she was constructing in the backyard, our little overachiever had herself another nest (yes, it was the same female), and this one was filled to capacity with two stubby-billed, adorable baby hummers.

I am not ashamed to admit that I cried. It was so spectacularly magical to have not one but two hummingbird nests in our small yard—and to discover them on the same day.

The realization that this tiny bird would be actively building another nest while raising two demanding "kids" at the same time—all on her own—was such emotional overload for me. It was the best day.
—*Kimberly Kaufman*

Hungry, Hungry Hummingbirds

10 feeding tricks to keep your backyard buzzing with nectar-loving birds.

A classic plastic feeder is all it takes to lure this male Anna's and other hummingbirds.

A ruby-throat uses its pumplike tongue to sip nectar from a zinnia bloom.

Red-Eye Flights

Hummingbirds are attracted to bright colors, especially red. The eyes of hummers have high concentrations of cones that heighten their ability to see reds and yellows, while dulling shades of blue. Curiously, while red is a clue for them to find food, that alone won't keep the birds coming back for more. When researchers altered the nectar levels in flowers, hummingbirds quickly keyed in on the blooms that offered elevated levels of nutrients, even if they weren't red.

No. 1 Food

Premade concentrate is available in stores, but there is no need for red dye. Clear nectar is best. It is also easy to make your own hummingbird cocktails. Stick to water and white table sugar in a 4-1 ratio—the sweeteners spoil quickly. Heating the water helps dissolve the sugar. Be sure to cool it down so it's not too hot or cold, but just right.

Refresh Early and Often

To save time, make larger batches of sugar water, which will keep for about a week in the refrigerator. Feeders should be refreshed at least every two or three days—and more frequently in warm weather. This isn't because hummingbirds are being picky. Replacing it often will keep contamination and mold growth down. Placing feeders in shady areas may slow down the growth of gunk, too, but you should still refill regularly.

IN MANY WAYS, a hummingbird is the Goldilocks of the bird world. Pleasing one or more of these finicky fliers takes a fair bit of know-how, but when everything is just right, they make themselves at home in your neighborhood. From the ruby-throat in the East to the many species found in the West, hosting these beauties is well worth the extra effort.

Hummingbirds are typically very territorial, but these two male Anna's are sharing nicely.

Watch as hummingbirds snatch tiny insects in midair.

Squeaky-Clean Stop

Clean feeders are a critical part of maintaining a hummingbird-friendly backyard. Feeders don't need to be rinsed every time you fill them but they should be washed and sterilized many times throughout the season. Some people find it easiest to have an extra set of feeders to swap out. A quick cycle in the dishwasher shouldn't hurt anything, but scrubbing by hand will do. Toothbrushes work especially well for getting into those tiny feeding ports.

Plant a Feeder

Native plants function as a self-serve buffet to hummingbirds and native pollinators including bees, butterflies and even bats in some regions. Spring and fall migration are the best times to see hummingbirds, so choose plant species that bloom at different times throughout the season.

Splish Splash

Birdbaths appeal to hummingbirds, as do bird showers. Spinners and misters keep water flowing, and that's what catches their attention. The bonus: Movement cuts down on algae and mosquito larva growth in standing pools, all while attracting a variety of bird species. Hummers love to hover and dart in and out of the fine droplets of spray.

Strike a Perch Pose

Territorial by nature, many individuals like to watch over their turf from prominent perches. Using this to your advantage, it is possible to direct the backyard traffic by strategically placing landing pads. As an added benefit, this sets the stage for capturing stunning photos of perching and preening birds. Decorative perches and swings are available, but any old branch works.

Make a Buffet

Multiple feeding stations may reduce some territorial skirmishes. Try feeders in the front and backyards. Even placing just two feeders in opposite ends of your space is beneficial. It's impossible for the dominant individual to be in both places at once, so other birds have a chance to slurp up a bit of sugar water before getting chased off.

Place a swing near feeders where ruby-throats, like this one, and other fliers can perch.

Invite Insects

Hummingbirds can't survive on sugar water alone. Insects are an essential part of their diet. They often pluck these protein-packed snacks right out of the air. A healthy landscape does double duty, serving as a food source and a nesting site. Spiders, for example, are a tasty treat, and their silky webs make perfect nesting material. Sticky, stretchy and resilient, the silk allows the nest to expand as tiny hummingbird babies grow.

Interlopers

If you've created a welcoming hummingbird station, you've rolled out the welcome mat for other guests as well. Ant moats and bee guards help exclude insect invaders. Feeders without perches make it more difficult for other birds to access the sugar water. While it's always nice to see orioles and larger birds, too, sometimes they tip feeders, leading to spills that attract unwanted visitors.

Fluttering Along

The traits that make hummingbirds tick.

Large eyes pick up as many colors as human eyes do, plus ultraviolet light

Lead edges of wings create tornado-like vortexes to help with hovering

Tongues act as thin pumps that contract to draw in nectar

Dainty feet for perching only; hummingbirds don't walk or hop

Sturdy tail feathers used like rudders to make hairpin turns

NECTAR SPECIALISTS

No fliers are as well equipped to extract nectar as hummingbirds. With long, thin bills and tongues that lick up to 13 times a second, their mouths alone make them impressive. But the awe doesn't stop there—they are among the few birds with the ability to steadily hover and fly backward, allowing them to easily move from flower to flower.

A rufous hummingbird sips nectar from a Pride of Madeira bloom

How do you keep your feeders busy with activity?

Attract more of these tiny jeweled fliers with top-notch reader advice.

Keep your feeders at the ready to support early birds and late arrivals! I hang my feeders as early as St. Patrick's Day and take them inside on Halloween.

Rochelle Backer ARLINGTON, TENNESSEE

If your hummingbirds are aggressive, it's best to place several feeders around your yard, preferably in the corners so territorial birds won't be able to guard all the feeders at once.

Toni Hall SOUTH LAKE TAHOE, CALIFORNIA

The best way to attract hummingbirds is to keep feeders clean. Use only boiled water and sugar, and hang in shady areas so it doesn't spoil.

Barbara Wilkinson GOLDEN, COLORADO

I use saucer feeders because they're easy to clean and don't drip.

Becky Sims MONTAGUE, CALIFORNIA

Make your own nectar. My birds seem to like the homemade stuff more than mixes.

Jackie Taylor HUBERT, NORTH CAROLINA

Black & Blue salvia is popular among ruby-throated hummingbirds.

Plant sweet peas or Black & Blue salvia under a window for a natural food source. They love darting from flower to flower.

Carolyn Lennart WARRENVILLE, ILLINOIS

WINGING IT

Anna's, like other hummingbirds, are unable to walk or hop with their small legs. To move even a fraction of an inch on a perch, they take off and land in their desired spot.

West Coast Cuties

Full feeders and fanciful flowers keep Anna's hummingbirds in backyards year-round.

A STOCKY, MEDIUM-SIZED HUMMINGBIRD, the Anna's has a straight, short bill and a broad tail that extends past the wings. With bold metallic greens above a gray belly, Anna's is the only North American hummingbird sporting a full reddish crown.

Males proudly display a brilliant magenta throat, called a gorget, and crown. If it appears to be more violet than rose in color, the bird could be a hybrid that is the result of mating between Anna's and Costa's hummingbirds.

Females have specks of pink-red on their throats, often forming a small gorget that is unusual for female hummingbirds. Their backs are a duller iridescent green, with drab gray underparts.

To attract a mate a male puts on an aerial display that starts with hovering a few yards in front of a female. He ascends above the treetops, then dives toward the ground, pulling up with a loud screech made by his tail feathers. He does the same to intimidate intruders (including people).

Males also sing to attract a mate, which is rare among northern temperate hummingbirds, though their squeaks and buzzes are hardly musical to the human ear.

Anna's hummingbirds breed in winter and spring. After mating, the female uses spider silk to bind together pieces of plants, hair, feathers and lichen to make a nest among twiggy branches of a tree or vine. Her two pearly eggs hatch in two weeks, and the chicks fledge three weeks later.

Anna's range and numbers have grown thanks to feeders and their attraction to both ornamental and native flowers. During the early 1900s, they were found primarily in northern Baja California and Southern California. The hummingbirds now reside as far north as British Columbia and sometimes wander north to Alaska. Their range also extends eastward into Arizona, Nevada, Utah and western Texas, though they've been spotted as far away as New York and Newfoundland.

The growing and blooming cycles of native coastal chaparral plants match the breeding and feeding habits of Anna's—critical pollinators in these ecosystems. This beneficial relationship is one reason Anna's are adapted to nesting in winter and early spring along the coast. At other seasons they may move to higher elevations in search of food, and some migrate east and west across California and Arizona.

Anna's eat insects like midges and leafhoppers. The high-protein diet might help them tolerate colder conditions in gardens, parks and streamside areas all along the West Coast year-round.

> "A male Anna's was turning on the charm to attract a female. He displayed his beautiful gorget feathers."
>
> **Lisa Swanson**
> MARICOPA, ARIZONA

COOL DOWN

The body temperature of an Anna's hummingbird is typically 107 degrees, but it can drop to 48 degrees when it goes into torpor, a kind of deep sleep, during cold weather. It takes about 20 minutes to "awaken."

FLYING HIGH

A male Anna's hummingbird zooms upward as much as 130 feet when performing his courtship display.

Purple Attraction

Grow a vibrant flower patch that any hummingbird will adore.

1

SUN LOVERS
Salvias come in a variety of colors and most prefer full sun, but some cultivars, like this Purple Majesty, tolerate part shade.

1 Salvia

SALVIA SPP., ZONES 3 TO 10

With as many as a thousand species, there's an ideal salvia for nearly every garden out there. Also known as sage, salvia displays long, thin flowers that hummingbirds love. Choose native varieties or seek out spectacular selections like Rockin' Deep Purple.

Why we love it: Pollinators go for salvias. You could plant an entire garden of salvia varieties, and it would hum with activity every day.

2 Hummingbird mint

AGASTACHE FOENICULUM, ZONES 4 TO 8

Also known as anise hyssop, this wildflower releases a sweet licorice fragrance when you brush against the leaves. Hummingbird mint is drought tolerant and thrives in well-draining, moist soils, where it grows up to 4 feet tall.

Why we love it: It's right there in the name! Hummingbirds visit the lavender flower spikes in droves. Butterflies also frequently indulge in this species.

3 Bee balm

MONARDA SPP., ZONES 3 TO 9

Bee balms come in a variety of shades, including the pleasing purples of cultivars like Pardon My Purple and Purple Rooster. It's an excellent choice for moist, rich soils, but bee balm is susceptible to mildew. Look for newer varieties bred for resistance.

Why we love it: Bee balm, also called bergamot, has a lovely citrusy scent and flavor, and can be used in tea or as a salad topping.

4 Beardtongue

PENSTEMON SPP., ZONES 3 TO 9

Tall spires of beardtongue, also called penstemon, are loaded with nectar-filled blooms that hummingbirds can't resist. Most varieties prefer dry or well-draining soil and don't tolerate soggy roots or clay. Give them plenty of sun to encourage strong, sturdy growth.

Why we love it: Beardtongue is native to North America, with many options for easy-to-grow species found in nearly every region.

5 Foxglove

DIGITALIS PURPUREA, ZONES 4 TO 8

Tall and sturdy spires full of blooms grow up to 5 feet tall from a central foliage rosette in spring. Keep foxglove consistently moist but in well-draining soil. Cut back wilted flower stalks to encourage a second flush in midsummer. All parts are poisonous, so carefully watch children and pets when they're around these plants. **Why we love it:** Foxglove's regal spikes attract hummingbirds but repel deer and rabbits.

6 Columbine

AQUILEGIA VULGARIS, ZONES 3 TO 8

Columbine flowers are uniquely lovely, and appear in spring around the same time as daffodils and tulips. The bell-shaped blossoms are backed by darker spurs that contain the nectar hummingbirds need. Columbines generally prefer partial shade. **Why we love it:** Columbines thrive in woodland wildflower gardens. For another burst of green, cut the plant back to encourage new foliage.

7 Petunia

PETUNIA HYBRIDS, ANNUAL

All summer gardens should have a few easygoing petunias to fill the sunny spots. They're available in a wide range of colors and patterns, some featuring impressive stripes and bicolored blooms. Cut petunias back in summer if they become leggy for improved flowering. **Why we love it:** Petunias are absolutely gorgeous trailing from hanging baskets and bring visiting hummers up to eye level.

Comma butterfly rests on butterfly bush

8 Aster

ASTER OR SYMPHYOTRICHUM SPP., ZONES 3 TO 10

Asters bear daisylike flowers that crowd the top of the stems, like those of New England aster, or branch out to the sides like the calico aster. Many bloom during hummingbird migration in late summer and fall. Asters usually like moist soil and plentiful sun.

Why we love it: Late season butterflies also love asters, especially when it's mixed with other plants, such as ironweed and goldenrod.

9 Butterfly bush

BUDDLEJA DAVIDII, ZONES 5 TO 9

Butterflies and hummers treasure the bright clusters of tiny florets on this small shrub. In cool climates, cut it back 4 to 6 inches from the ground in early spring. Gardeners in warmer areas should also cut back the bush to manage its size. Buddleja is invasive in some areas; check before planting.

Why we love it: The bush's light and sweet fragrance will remind you of spring all season long.

Azurri Blue Satin rose of Sharon

10 Rose of Sharon

HIBISCUS SYRIACUS, ZONES 4 TO 9

Whether you grow it as a luscious shrub or groom it into a tree, rose of Sharon boasts big blooms that last only a day. Fortunately, this popular performer flowers continuously from midsummer to fall when planted in full sun. Watch for Japanese beetles, which can cause serious foliage damage.

Why we love it: One very pretty cultivar, Blue Bird, has a contrasting deep burgundy center and bright white stamen.

Plant a Hot Spot

Fuel late-season visitors with these fall-blooming nectar picks.

A ruby-throated hummingbird sips nectar from tube-shaped cardinal flowers.

HUMMINGBIRD HABITS IN AUTUMN aren't what they used to be—and that could be a good thing if you'd like to see more of the speedy little fliers whizzing around your backyard later in the season.

"Things have shifted," says John Rowden, director of community conservation at the National Audubon Society. Ruby-throated hummingbirds, the only species found in most of the eastern half of the country, used to depart colder regions in September. Now some of them are lingering into October, with sightings in November and even December, far outside their usual wintering range.

Also on the rise across much of the country are fall sightings of western hummingbirds like the coppery rufous, Calliope, Anna's and others.

Scientists can't say for sure what is causing the recent shift. But John notes that late fall hummingbirds "are actually spending a fair bit of time at feeders, guarding a feeder as a very valuable resource."

While sugar-water feeders will provide an easy feast, hummingbirds often take breaks from a feeder to visit nearby flowers or snap up tiny insects. And if a feisty hummer declares, "This feeder is all mine," late-blooming plants give others a chance to eat.

So when summer's most sweltering heat is behind you, it's important to have planted food sources that will provide snacks through the early fall rush and keep thriving, even after frost.

Nasturtium

Black-chinned at coral honeysuckle vine

Ruby-throated at blue anise sage

Jupiter's beard

Painted lady butterfly on Walker's Low catmint

Plant a Fall Feast

Low-maintenance flowers peak around autumn and bloom until latecomers have passed through. Plant these sun-loving beauties in early summer, and watch them blossom and thrive when the migrating hummingbirds reach your yard—whether that's August, September, October or November.

Walker's Low catmint

NEPETA RACEMOSA 'WALKER'S LOW', ZONES 4 TO 9

Beautiful, reliable Walker's Low creates a 2- to 3-foot mound of flowers from May to November. Give it a haircut to slow down the blooms and fix floppy growth. Just cut about halfway down the stem.

Blue Fortune anise hyssop

AGASTACHE, ZONES 3 TO 8

A magnet for late summer bumblebees, butterflies and other pollinators, this sturdy, upright perennial blooms well into fall. Hybrids are less aggressive, but natives are biennial, self-seeding and just as pretty.

Edging lobelia

LOBELIA ERINUS, ANNUAL

"Lobelias can be very good," says John. He gives a strong vote to two native varieties: great blue lobelia (*L. siphilitica*) and cardinal flower (*L. cardinalis*). Annual edging lobelia, the popular container plant, blooms much longer than those perennials, making it ideal for extended fall color and nectar. Shear it back when it gets straggly to encourage reblooming.

Pineapple sage

SALVIA ELEGANS, ZONES 8 TO 10 OR ANNUAL

The hummingbird traffic at this late bloomer is incredible, and so is the size it reaches in a single season—up to 3 feet tall and wide! But growing pineapple sage is a bit of a gamble. A frost before it reaches full fiery bloom could kill it. Be sure to throw a bedsheet over the plant whenever frost is in the forecast.

Salvia

SALVIA, ZONES 7 TO 11 OR ANNUAL

All salvias are superb hummingbird plants. Two varieties, Indigo Spires and blue anise sage, zoom to 6 feet tall where they are winter hardy, and deer usually ignore their fragrant leaves.

Coral honeysuckle

LONICERA SEMPERVIRENS, ZONES 4 TO 9

This semi-evergreen vine is a top pick among native plants that make hummers happy. Crowned with a mass of red-orange flowers from summer through early fall, it often puts out even more new flowers into late fall.

Nasturtium

TROPAEOLUM MAJUS, ANNUAL

Poke the big round seeds of these easy annuals into window boxes, containers and the front of your garden. Cool fall weather invigorates the plants, inducing a bounty of new blossoms that survive until the first frost!

Jupiter's beard

CENTRANTHUS RUBER, ZONES 5 TO 8

Hummingbirds love hot pink blooms, and this sprawling perennial keeps pumping out clusters of tiny bright flowers from summer through very late fall. Snip off fluffy seed head clusters to keep it blooming.

GET GROWING

Fill out your garden and any containers with verbenas, snapdragons and edging lobelia, which keep blooming through light frosts.

Snowberry clearwing moth at great blue lobelia

Blue Fortune anise hyssop

Ruby-throated at pineapple sage

CHAPTER 3

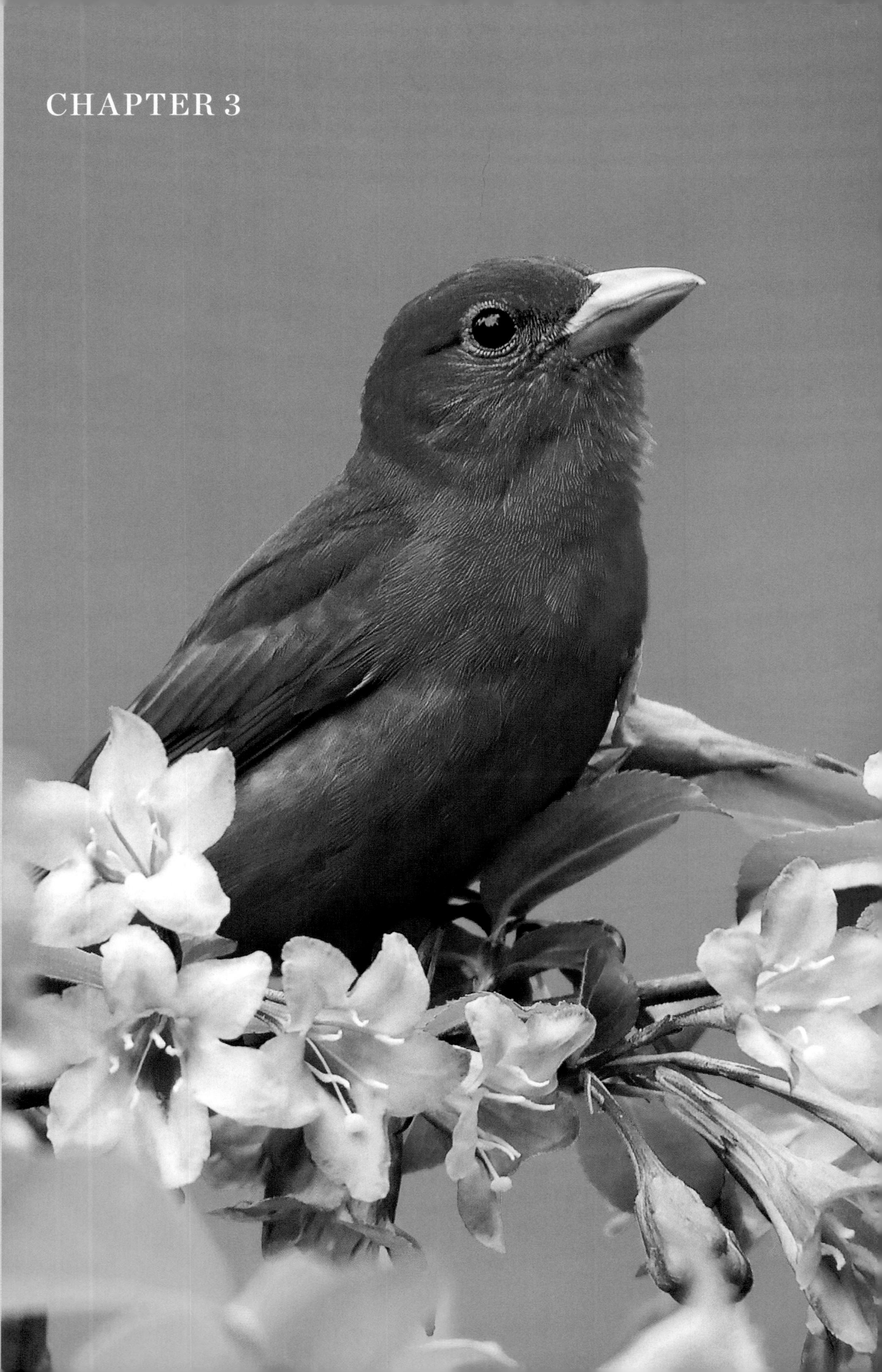

Birds
In-Depth

Take a closer look at species you might not normally see, and learn about bird behavior.

Black-and-white

The Wonderful World of Warblers

Meet the colorful insect eaters that zip and zoom around your yard, often going unnoticed.

Black-throated
green

WARBLER MIX-UP

Many warblers are brightly patterned, often sporting various hues of yellow. Their actions are quick and sporadic. As you're scanning tall foliage, remember that the lemony hues and twitchy behaviors of flycatchers, vireos, goldfinches or kinglets look a lot like those of warblers!

Magnolia

LIKE MULTICOLORED ORNAMENTS dotting the tree branches, warblers dazzle and delight as they arrive in the U.S. and Canada each spring. They fly north at night from Central and South America and the Caribbean, dropping into the nearest treetops at dawn to find food. They're searching for insects and water, so although you won't see them at your feeders, they still might show up in your yard. Here are just a few of the most likely garden guests.

Yellow-rumped

Nashville

Black-and-White

Resembling an avian zebra, the black-and-white warbler creeps up and down tree trunks like a nuthatch as it probes bark crevices for moth and butterfly larvae, beetles and spiders. It breeds in northern and eastern North America, and it can be seen in woodland habitats during migration, mostly east of the Rockies.

Black-Throated Green

You might hear this warbler before you see it as it gives a buzzy *zee zee zee zoo zee* from eastern treetops. A common migrant, it has a deep black throat, yellow head, olive-green back and two white wing bars. The black-throated green nests in northern coniferous forests and mixed forests in the Appalachians.

Nashville

This bird was named when it was discovered in Nashville, Tennessee, but it breeds much farther north in bogs and coniferous woods, among other habitats. During migration the Nashville often is seen in thickets and small trees. Identify it by its gray head, solid white eye ring and yellow body.

Magnolia

A fairly common midseason migrant in the East, the magnolia has a yellow throat and breast boldly streaked with black, a blue head and white wing bars. Ornithologist Alexander Wilson named the species after discovering it in a magnolia tree in Mississippi. It actually frequents all kinds of trees during migration, often hanging out at the tips of branches, and nests in boreal forests.

Yellow-Rumped

One of the earliest and most abundant migrants, the male yellow-rumped has a lemon-colored rear end, shoulders and cap. In the East, its throat is white; in the West, it's yellow. Females have duller colors and migrate later. Yellow-rumpeds nest in northern coniferous forests, but they eat suet at feeders. In early spring, dozens or more of these butter-butts can be found together in one area.

Wilson's

ATTRACT MORE WARBLERS

These birds can't resist the sound of dripping water! Add a dripper or small fountain to a birdbath or pond. Or place a trickling hose in a secluded spot and watch them drink and bathe. Plant trees like oaks that attract the insects and larvae they eat to help draw them in.

American redstart

Wilson's

Much more common in the West but found nationwide during migration, a Wilson's warbler is easy to identify with its lemon yellow body and black cap. It hangs out in lower levels of vegetation, picking caterpillars and insects from the leaves and branches. The Wilson's warbler breeds in Canada and the western U.S., typically in shrubby areas near streams. It's one of the last migrating warblers to arrive.

American Redstart

The American redstart fans out its brightly colored tail, a notable behavior that makes it easy to identify. Males are black with orange patches on the sides, wings and tails. Females and immature birds are mostly gray and yellow or yellowish orange. One of the most common migrant warblers, the redstart winters from Florida to South America and breeds in the eastern and northern U.S. and Canada. Its variable song often ends in a sharp *shew*.

Palm

Palm

Pumping its tail up and down constantly like a palm tree swaying in the wind, this warbler sports a rust-colored cap and yellow eyebrow stripe. While palm warblers nest in the boreal forest, during migration it's easy to see them as they feed in short to medium vegetation across the eastern U.S.

Chestnut-Sided

Some describe the song lyrics of this eastern migrant as *pleased to meetcha*. It has a yellow crown and chestnut sides, and like many warbler species, it hovers underneath a leaf to grab a caterpillar or sallies out from a branch to snatch an insect. John James Audubon said he had seen only five chestnut-sided warblers in his lifetime, but they are more common now.

Chestnut-sided

The Truth About Tanagers

These bright songbirds dot the treetops from coast to coast every summer. Here are the secrets behind their hidden identities.

Adult male summer tanagers, like this one on a weigela shrub, are the only completely red birds in North America.

A FLASH OF RED OR YELLOW among dense foliage, followed by a husky song floating down from the treetops—it's a common performance tanagers put on every summer. Four birds with tanager in the name are widespread in North American forests, and the males are among the most colorful songbirds. One or more of these species is found practically everywhere in the Lower 48 states and southern Canada in summer, along with another occasional visitor.

Tanagers dine on insects and small fruits. This scarlet tanager has a mouthful of mulberry.

Western tanagers, found in the western half of North America, sport bold, vibrant hues that resemble a flame.

In addition to vibrant, flashy colors that light up a forest, tanagers share a distinctive bill shape. Moderately thick, it's ideal for feeding on large insects and small fruits. Their whistled songs and sharp, distinctive callnotes ring out as they move slowly and deliberately through the high branches of the forest canopy.

The most surprising thing about North American tanagers is that they are not tanagers at all—meaning they don't actually belong to the tanager family. Scientists recently determined that the five birds mentioned here are more closely related to cardinals, grosbeaks and buntings. But their names have become so well established for so long that name changes to "scarlet cardinal" or "summer grosbeak" are extremely unlikely.

Scarlet

The most famous and recognizable member of the group is the scarlet tanager. An adult male is unmistakable in summer: brilliant scarlet red, with black wings and tail. The female is more subtly colored, sporting soft yellow-green with darker wings and tail. It makes sense for her to be camouflaged, because she builds the nest—usually high in an oak tree—and incubates the eggs. However, the male scarlet does step up to help feed the young.

Throughout summer, scarlet tanagers are widespread in the eastern states and southeastern Canada, mainly in forests dominated by oaks. They spend winters in lowland rain forest areas of the Amazon basin in South America.

Before migrating south in fall, males perform a costume change, molting their bright red feathers and replacing them with yellow-green tones like those of the female. Males go through another molt in late winter before heading north, so when they reach the eastern woods, they have the brilliant colors you know and love. Scarlets announce their annual arrivals with a hoarse, whistled song, like a robin with a sore throat.

Summer

All across the southern United States, from California to the Carolinas, a slow, lazy, robinlike song is a sure sign that a summer tanager is present. Even if it isn't singing, you may hear its characteristic callnote, a snappy *pick-i-tuck*.

Summer tanagers sound the same across their range, but they favor different habitats in different regions. In the Southeast they are common in oak and pine forests, while those in the Southwest concentrate in tall cottonwood trees along lowland rivers. In fall they migrate to tropical wintering grounds that stretch all the way from Mexico to South America.

Contrary to what the moniker might suggest, and unlike the male scarlet tanager that is red only in spring and summer, the male summer tanager keeps his bright colors in all seasons. A nickname for summer tanager is "beebird," because it eats many wasps and bees, sometimes catching them in midair.

THE REAL TANAGERS

In the American tropics, tanagers are some of the most brilliantly hued songbirds. A traveler to some parts of South America might see more than 30 kinds of tanagers displaying a brilliant rainbow of every color imaginable. The medium-sized songbirds have thick bills, and some of them look similar to birds like the scarlet tanager or summer tanager. Researchers now know they're not related.

A hepatic tanager is more of a brick red color than the true red of its relatives.

Western

West of the Great Plains lives another tanager with a more varied color pattern. A male western tanager is a flashy bird with a bright yellow body, red head, and black tail and wings. Its wings have yellow or white bars. Females are a paler yellow with gray wings, but they show the same wing bars.

Western tanagers spend the winter mostly in forests of Central America. During migration, they may stop over anywhere, from western backyards to the desert. For the summer, they head to cool forests of pine, spruce or fir, from high mountains of the Southwest all the way to northwestern Canada.

Hepatic and Flame-Colored

In mountain pine forests of the Southwest, from southern Colorado to Arizona and western Texas, a pair of tanagers—a red male and yellow female—might look like summer tanagers at first glance. But the male is a more brick red color, not rose-red like a summer tanager, and the female is a richer yellow with gray cheeks. These are hepatic tanagers, members of a tropical species that's found all the way south to Argentina. Hepatic tanagers are barely migratory, just withdrawing from the northern edge of their range in fall, and a few can be found in Arizona even in winter.

A fifth type of tanager is a rare visitor. The flame-colored tanager was never found north of the Mexican border until 1985, when a male appeared in Arizona's Chiricahua Mountains. Several have been found since, in mountains of southern Arizona and western Texas.

Whether it's a rarity like a flame-colored or a more widespread species like a scarlet or summer, any sighting of a tanager will add color and excitement to the time you spend outdoors.

ATTRACTING TANAGERS

These birds are choosy about nesting sites, so they won't stay for the summer unless you live close to forest land. But passing migrants might show up almost anywhere in spring or fall. Entice tanagers with fruits like bananas, orange halves or sliced watermelon. A water source is the best way to attract them, especially a birdbath with a dripper or small fountain that creates the sound of trickling water.

The flame-colored tanager was first seen in the U.S. in 1985.

Desert Birds

You'll be amazed by the surprising ways
they survive and thrive in dry country.

IT'S CHILLY AT DAWN in the desert, even though blazing heat will arrive before midday. To the east, stark outlines of cactus and thorny trees stand against the growing light. And on all sides, the air is alive with the songs of birds.

People are often delighted to learn that the deserts of the Southwest provide excellent birding. These arid lands support a rich variety of birds, including some kinds that live nowhere else.

Life in the Dry Zones

Although water is essential for survival, many desert birds are adapted to exist with very little of it. Black-throated sparrows, found all over the Southwest, go weeks or even months at a time without drinking any water at all. They get enough moisture from consuming seeds and insects. Where doves live in desert country, they satisfy most of their moisture needs by eating cactus fruits. But they also fly long distances mornings and evenings to visit streams, ponds or other water sources.

Some widespread birds found in other habitats also live in deserts. For example, northern cardinals are usually thought of as backyard and forest birds of the eastern states, but they live in southern Arizona, too. Because they need more water, cardinals are found primarily along rivers and streams throughout the desert. A close relative, the pyrrhuloxia—a gray and red beauty often called a desert cardinal—lives along the same streams, also moving into much drier zones that cardinals avoid.

The sharply patterned black-throated sparrow (this one is on a cholla cactus) is a true desert bird, often going many days without water and living long distances from a water source.

Gambel's quail are at home in urban and suburban areas, wandering into parks and even backyards to eat sunflower seeds, millet and cracked corn from platform or ground feeders.

A Different Menu

Food is sometimes scarce in arid country, and birds have their own ways of coping. One of the most remarkable southwestern species, the greater roadrunner, eats just about anything it can catch. Roadrunners are famous for eating snakes (even rattlesnakes!) and lizards, but they also go after insects, spiders, scorpions, mice and even small birds. While rather like birds of prey that dash around on foot, they actually belong to the cuckoo family.

Costa's hummingbird, the only member of its family adapted to living in North American deserts, likes flower nectar just as much as its relatives do. But flowers are scarce in dry habitats, so this hummingbird moves with the seasons, migrating east and west in search of flowering plants. Another mobile bird, the glossy black phainopepla, feeds on berries, and it travels from streamside thickets in summer to clumps of mistletoe in the desert at other seasons.

Both the curve-billed thrasher (right) and cactus wren (far right) are skilled at slipping through the sharp spines of cactus thickets, choosing to build nests and raise their young there.

Greater roadrunners are not picky eaters. Almost anything they catch in the desert, including rattlesnakes, may become dinner.

Spiny Shelters

In the sparse, open vegetation of the desert, birds are creative when hiding their nests. One popular choice is a type of cactus called cholla, which looks like a short jumble of stout branches covered with sharp spines. Humans have a hard time even walking past a cholla without being poked. Many birds build their nests deep within the center of this cactus, and they fly in and out hundreds of times without getting stuck.

The big, boldly marked cactus wren often chooses cholla as the site for its bulky nest. And the curve-billed thrasher, a yellow-eyed bird with a sharp *whit-wheet!* call, also favors cholla. In Arizona, a scientist once found a large cholla cactus containing five old cactus wren nests, four old thrasher nests, and another nest still occupied by a brand-new family of thrashers.

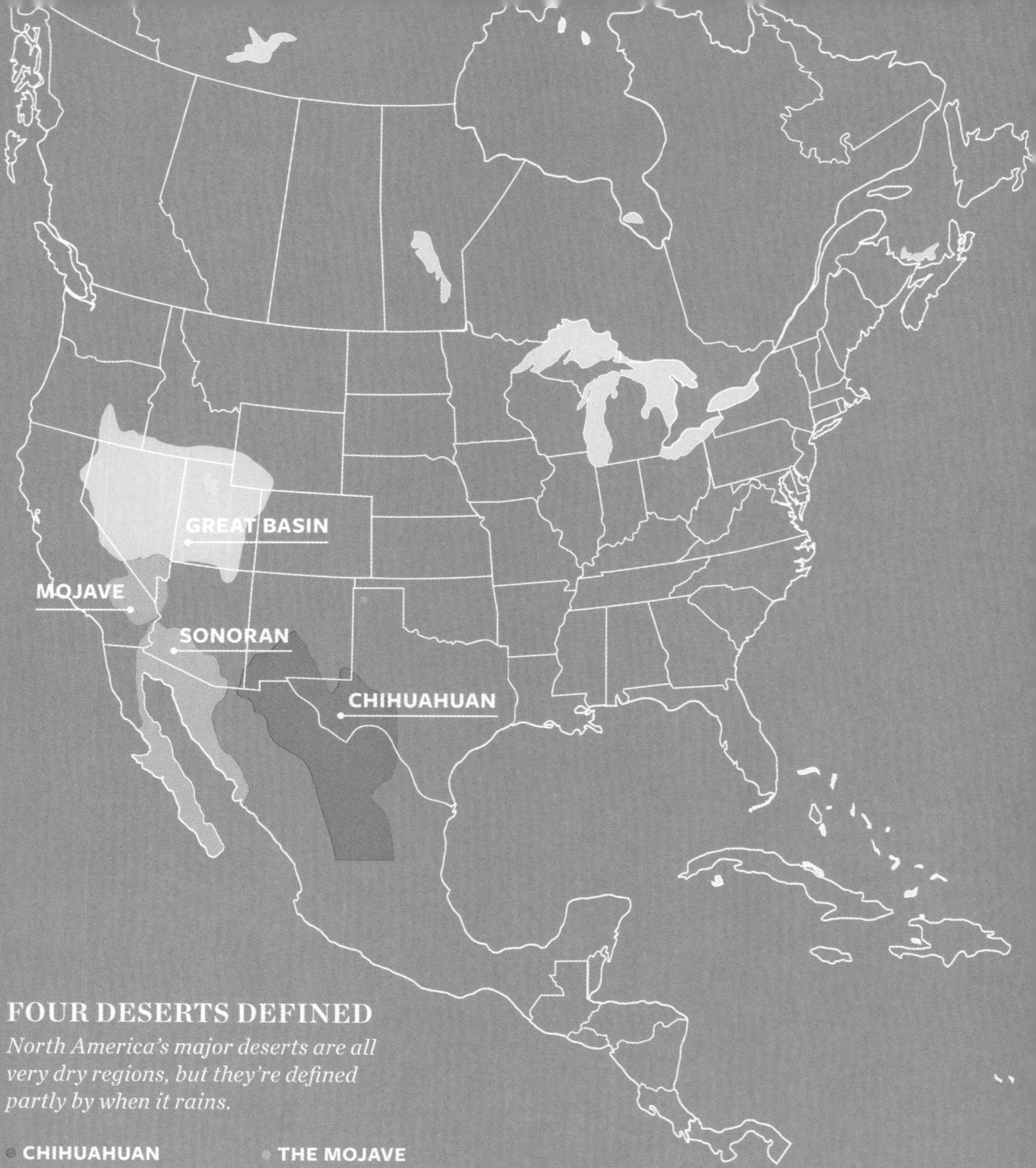

FOUR DESERTS DEFINED

North America's major deserts are all very dry regions, but they're defined partly by when it rains.

Map labels:
- GREAT BASIN
- MOJAVE
- SONORAN
- CHIHUAHUAN

- **CHIHUAHUAN DESERT** Rain falls mainly in summer and supports a sparse growth of grass, small bushes and scattered cactus in this desert, which covers large areas of western Texas and New Mexico.

- **THE GREAT BASIN DESERT** Mostly in Nevada and Utah, this sagebrush country gets most of its precipitation in the form of winter snow.

- **THE MOJAVE DESERT** Rain falls occasionally in winter here; this desert is mostly in southeastern California and southern Nevada.

- **SONORAN DESERT** Summer and winter are considered rainy seasons, which means this southern Arizona desert supports the most plant life, with a wide variety of cactus, shrubs and short trees.

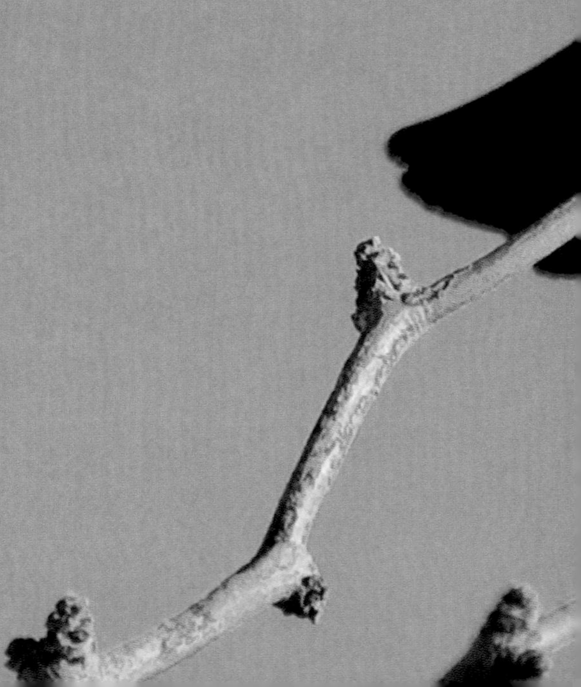

Phainopeplas rarely drink water. These unique-looking crested birds get most of the water they need to survive from eating mistletoe berries.

Many desert birds place their nests on the ground or in short thorny trees like mesquites or acacias. Another drought lover, the yucca plant, which looks like a bunch of green daggers sticking out from a central stalk, is a favorite nesting site for the colorful Scott's oriole.

The most distinctive nesting site is the saguaro, a giant cactus with upcurved arms that stands up to 60 feet tall. Woodpeckers climb the saguaro trunk as if it were a tree, and they dig holes in it for nesting cavities. The gilded flicker and Gila woodpecker, well adapted to desert life, usually create a new nest hole every time they're ready to raise a family. Later, these cavities serve as nesting sites for other birds like purple martins (yes, there are martins in the desert), brown-crested flycatchers and small owls. The elf owl, the tiniest owl in the world, often lives in these holes in the largest cactuses. As darkness falls, an elf owl may sit at the entrance to its nest, making little yelping and chuckling sounds, before it flies out to hunt for its next insect meal.

Urban Discoveries

In southwestern cities and towns, the best landscape plants are natives, already adapted to local conditions. People who fill their gardens with native desert plants will discover that native birds move right in. The verdin, a tiny gray sprite with a yellow head, flits through backyards throughout the dry zones. Colorful Gambel's quail strut into suburbs and parks. White-winged doves are often more common in southwestern towns than they are out in more rural habitats. So it's possible to do some desert birding even without a long trek into the wilderness.

Whether you live in the Southwest or you're visiting from far away, if you get a chance to explore desert country, you'll find that these arid lands hold many treasures—including the feathered kind.

Perfectly Imperfect Plumage

Discover why birds develop surprising and irregular feather colors.

A stunning sight, this black-chinned hummingbird is leucistic, which means it's missing pigments in its feathers.

The melanin pigments in this bald eagle's feathers are low, resulting in an appearance that's pale brown instead of a darker brown.

SEEING BIRDS PARADE such colorful feathers is one of the greatest joys in watching winged visitors. The hues and patterns of their plumage are both decorative and practical, making them gaudy enough to attract mates or subtle enough to blend into their surroundings. Plumage is also a reliable way for bird-watchers to recognize different species.

Sometimes, though, a bird has a very unusual feather pattern—one that is not quite how it's supposed to look or doesn't match up with the pictures in a guidebook. Such striking and surprising colors have a number of causes. If you know what makes these odd variations possible, it's exciting, not confusing, when you spot one.

Flashes of White

A flock of robins gathers on the lawn and among them is a bird that looks similar, but with big patches of white. A flock of house sparrows flies past, and there's an all-white bird with them. Are they some rare visitors?

No, they're just individuals of the same kind that lack normal pigments in their feathers.

Most of the black, gray, brown and reddish brown tones in feathers are created by pigments called melanins. If these pigments are missing, feathers may grow in pure white. Birds might have just a few white feathers, large random spots of them—or they might look completely white. All of these individuals are known as leucistic. Their appearance may throw you off at first, but with careful study, you can identify most by their shape and behavior, and if they're flocking with others of their own kind.

A leucistic female northern cardinal shows touches of red in all the usual places, but the dark brown pigments are absent, especially on her head.

Splotchy white birds are sometimes called partial albinos, but scientists disagree on whether this is a valid term. A true albino bird lacks all pigments, including in its eyes. So it would have white feathers and pink eyes (from blood vessels showing through). Genuine albinos rarely live long in the wild, so birders don't see them often. It's generally safe to assume that a white or partly white bird is leucistic.

In contrast, while a lack of melanin leads to white feathers, it is also possible for birds to have an excess of dark pigment. Extra dark, or melanistic, individuals are fairly common in some hawk species, and it's part of their normal variation. For most songbirds, however, melanistic plumages are very rare.

This 1-year-old male indigo bunting has molted into spring plumage—a patchy mix of brown and blue.

A Range of Hues

Red, orange and yellow feathers are usually created by other kinds of pigments called carotenoids, which are often independent of melanins. So a leucistic red-winged blackbird might have white plumage where melanin is missing from the black feathers but still show typical red and yellow pigment in the wings. The carotenoid colors often show odd variations, too, as in the rare male northern cardinals that are bright yellow instead of red.

Diet affects carotenoid pigments. For example, male house finches are usually bright red on the chest, but if they have a poor diet, their new feathers grow in orange and yellow. And if cedar waxwings eat the fruits from certain exotic plants, the tips of their tail feathers are known to turn red instead of the usual yellow.

BALDING BIRDS

If you've ever spotted a northern cardinal or blue jay with a mostly bald head, the bird isn't sick—don't worry! It is simply suffering from tiny parasites that cause some feathers to fall out. Most birds survive and grow back a full head of feathers in a few weeks.

Costume Change

Sometimes birds show unique color patterns for a while simply because they're changing from one set of feathers to another.

As a very general rule, a healthy wild bird replaces all its feathers at least once a year, just a few at a time, in a process called molt. The new feathers are often the same colors as the ones they're replacing, so the effect isn't obvious. But some species change colors with the seasons, or as they become adults. When those birds are partway through the molt, they can look very odd, with patterns unlike any picture in a field guide.

Look for male American goldfinches to see an example of the process. In spring and fall they molt their head and body feathers, going from drab, buffy brown to brilliant gold and then back again. The process takes at least a couple of weeks and while it's happening, they wear an ever-changing coat of color.

Something similar happens with other birds that change with the seasons. Adult male indigo buntings are blue in summer, and mostly brown in winter, and a mix when they're in their first year or in molt. Male scarlet tanagers trade their vibrant summer red for a winter costume of olive green, and they wear a mix of both in between. Adult male summer tanagers are bright red all year, but 1-year-old males are unevenly splotched as adult red starts to replace their baby olive.

Temporary Flair

Sometimes a bird sports unusual colors simply because birds are...well, messy. They get into things and get discolored. It may be obvious, like when a wading bird has mud on its belly. But the stains come from their diet too. Birds feeding on ripe berries or small fruits may have a face stained blue, purple or black. Birds that prefer nectar can be dusted with flower pollen. It's common to see a hummingbird with tints of yellow or orange on its face where pollen has stuck to its feathers.

Whatever the cause for discoloration, some birds just don't follow the dress code. Finding such a unique individual is a highlight for anyone who loves the variety of birdlife.

The Sequence of Spring Migration

From early arrivals like blackbirds to latecomers like flycatchers, find out when your favorite fliers will pass through.

Red-winged
blackbirds, like
this colorful male,
are among the
earliest spring
migrants.

Compared to other ducks, blue-winged teal are one of the latest species to take off for their breeding grounds each spring.

EVERY YEAR, A GRAND PARADE sweeps northward across the continent. Vast numbers of individuals take part, but they aren't marching up Main Street—they are spreading out from coast to coast, and even offshore. This famous procession is the spring migration of birds.

No matter where you are, the phenomenon lasts for months. Along the southern border it starts in January, while in the far north you might not see movement until March or even later. One thing is true everywhere: Certain birds come early in the order of migration, others much later. If you know what to expect, it's easy to plan your birding adventures.

Of the species that famously lead the way, most spend winter in the southern states, moving north as early as possible. Red-winged blackbirds and common grackles are good examples. Tough, adaptable birds that feed on almost anything, they can survive the risk of heading into cold regions.

However, not all of these early fliers travel short distances. Purple martins spend the first part of winter in South America but start their trek early, with advance scouts reaching Florida and Texas by the middle of January. In the far West, rufous and Allen's hummingbirds that

wintered in Mexico move north up the California coast by early February.

Next come the waterfowl—ducks, geese and swans—that have abandoned the coldest climates because most can't survive for long when all the water is frozen. But as soon as ponds and lakes begin to thaw in late winter, some waterfowl push north. By the first of March, flocks of pintails, wigeons, mallards and green-winged teal pulse into the northern states. Meanwhile, their numbers start to dwindle on southern lakes and bays as wintering waterfowl move on.

If you spot open water in early spring, look for grebes and great blue herons. Sandhill cranes also migrate early, and their wild, grating cries may drift down from the sky on any day at the edge of spring.

While water birds splash into freshly thawed ponds, sparrows arrive in fields and thickets. Native species such as song, fox and savannah

SHOREBIRD ITINERARY

They travel north throughout spring, so always check the water's edge for an ever-changing cast of characters.

FEBRUARY: Killdeers, American woodcocks

MARCH: Pectoral sandpipers, Wilson's snipes

APRIL: Greater and lesser yellowlegs

MAY: Semipalmated sandpipers, dunlins

EARLY JUNE: Ruddy turnstones, white-rumped sandpipers

The American golden-plover reaches the southern states by early March and the northern states by late March.

sparrows march northward as early as possible, feeding on weed seeds around the brushy areas. Some hardy insect eaters like ruby-crowned kinglets and brown creepers start migrating before most adult insects are active; they seek out insect eggs and larvae hiding in twigs or bark.

The excitement of migration kicks into high gear when large numbers of songbirds flying up from the tropics arrive. Hundreds of species spend the winter mostly south of our borders, and when they finally return, they fill the woods with color and song.

For many birders, warblers are the stars. Though there are more than 50 kinds, the small, active, brightly hued birds are difficult to see as they flit and zip among foliage. But they are worth the effort. Because warblers feed mainly on insects, they travel when they can rely on warm temperatures. Their peak flight is in April in the southern states and in May farther north. On the right spring morning at favored spots in the eastern states, it's possible to catch sight of 20 or more species of warblers.

When the warblers burst onto the scene, other migrants arrive with them. House wrens and gray catbirds come to lurk in thickets, while shy brown thrushes hop around in deep shade on the ground. Brilliantly colored birds like rose-breasted grosbeaks, orioles, tanagers and buntings dot the treetops. The peak of spring migration is a magical time, with endless potential for variety.

In most places, migration starts off slowly, builds to a crescendo in late spring and then trails off, but a few birds consistently come in after peak time. Most members of the flycatcher family show up late in the season, and with good reason: They feed on insects caught in midair, and the weather has to be warm before bugs start flying around. That also could explain the relatively late arrival of the common nighthawk, another aerial insect eater. And season's end is the best time to look for yellow-billed cuckoo and black-billed cuckoo, which munch on large caterpillars.

Spring migration is a great show from beginning to end, and it's free to watch. So grab your binoculars, get to your favorite bird-watching spot and enjoy the beautiful bird parade.

Prothonotary warblers (this one is on a bottle brush plant) are among the first of varied warblers to fly north.

Clowns of the Sea

Get to know puffins, the social, pint-size northern birds.

Atlantic puffins are the only puffin species with dark steel-blue triangles on the base of their beaks.

10 Standing 10 inches tall, Atlantic puffins weigh about a pound. Their feathers resemble a crisp tuxedo and offset a comical orange-striped beak.

5 It takes several years for puffins to mature and breed. At about 5 years old, they choose a partner that they mate with year after year.

1973 Atlantic puffins disappeared from colonies in southern Maine due to overhunting, but were reintroduced to Eastern Egg Rock starting in 1973 as part of Audubon's Project Puffin. Over 1,900 chicks were transplanted to re-establish the colony.

20 Most puffins live into their 20s. Researchers don't know the exact average age because puffins tend to live longer than tracking bands last.

62 On average, puffins catch and hold on to 10 fish for each trip to the sea. They use their tongues to secure the fish against their jagged palate, allowing them to bring more food back to their nests. One puffin in Britain was spotted with an astonishing 62 fish in its mouth at once.

200 Atlantic puffins dive 200 feet—often in half-minute plunges—but typically hunt in shallower waters for small fish, including sand lance, sprat, herring, hake and cod.

4 There are four species of puffins: Atlantic, horned, tufted and (despite the misleading name) rhinoceros auklets. They live along the northern coastlines of the Atlantic and Pacific oceans.

48 Despite their stocky builds, puffins pick up some serious speed! They flap their wings up to 400 beats a minute and fly 48-55 mph.

Weathering the Storm

Find out how powerful hurricanes impact songbirds, seabirds and more, and learn how you can help in the aftermath.

Birds that nest on beaches, like these black skimmers, are especially vulnerable when hurricanes roll in.

Hurricanes affect natural habitats of many bird species, including the sora rail (right), piping plover (below) and common tern (next page).

WHEN A POWERFUL STORM LIKE A HURRICANE spins toward the Atlantic or Gulf coasts, the first thought is dedicated to the people whose lives and homes are at risk. But when the storm passes, nature lovers can't help but wonder: What happens to birds during the storm?

Riding Out the Storm

Thanks to modern science, humans know when a tropical storm or hurricane is approaching. But birds have no such early warning system. Some scientists think they might be able to detect the low-pitched rumbling of a distant hurricane—a sound that is too low for humans to hear—but there's no proof so far. Birds probably notice the storm first as winds gradually increase over a matter of hours, bringing along scattered rain showers. Since wild birds live through storms all the time, they may not be bothered at first.

As winds increase, of course, all creatures take notice. Some large birds may fly away ahead of the storm, especially if they don't have nests with eggs or dependent young, but most species stay put and seek shelter. Woodpeckers may cling to the downwind side of a sturdy tree trunk or hide inside a hole. Cardinals, buntings and other songbirds find a spot deep in dense thickets, protected from the gales. Backyard birds take cover under sheds or on the lee side of houses, waiting for the worst to be over. Some won't

survive, unfortunately, but surprising numbers emerge unharmed after the storm passes.

Especially near the coast, a storm surge of rising waters may drive marsh birds up and out of their habitat. Seaside sparrows, rails and others are at great risk after they're flooded out of the marshes. Birds that nest on beaches and barrier islands, like terns, plovers and black skimmers, are especially vulnerable to hurricanes early in the season. By late summer their young will be flying strongly enough to escape, but if a storm

makes landfall before midsummer, many nests, eggs and young birds will be washed away.

Destruction of habitat does affect local wildlife long after a storm passes. When a major hurricane thunders through, forests and marshes may take years to recover. But the results aren't always all bad. Sometimes a storm that knocks out a few trees will open up a forest and make it more diverse, allowing for more variety of birdlife.

Migrants over Open Water

An autumn hurricane impacts many birds long before it reaches land. Any time after mid-August, large numbers of migratory birds are moving south over open water—across the Gulf of Mexico, or over the Atlantic as they head for the Caribbean or South America. When these birds get caught in the outer winds of a hurricane, they fly downwind until they end up in the calm eye at the storm's center.

Surrounded by a circular wall of battering winds, the tiny migrants keep flying within the eye as the hurricane moves west or north. After the storm comes ashore, they land and seek shelter, hiding while the outer winds of the hurricane lash over them. After the storm moves on, coastal areas may be carpeted with thousands of warblers, thrushes and other migrants that have been carried back to shore. They will have to rest, feed and build their strength before they continue their migration.

HOW TO HELP BIRDS AFTER A STORM

- Fill feeders with high-quality food such as suet cakes or sunflower seed.
- Offer water in a birdbath or other clean vessel.
- Check to see whether licensed wildlife rehabilitators are operating after the storm. If you find an injured bird after the worst weather passes, the rehab center may care for it, but keep in mind the center may be overwhelmed with other wildlife. If that's the case, ask if they need donations or help.
- Volunteer to help restore habitat, like coastal beaches.

Seabirds in the Eye

As a hurricane marches across the ocean, seabirds also concentrate in the eye of the storm. They get there the same way migrating land birds do: by flying downwind, in the increasing gales that spiral in toward the storm center, until they break out into the calmness of the eye. Then, rather than fight the winds, they stay within the eye as the storm moves.

If a hurricane travels inland, it may bring along some birds of the open ocean—such as shearwaters, tropicbirds, frigatebirds or sooty terns—eventually leaving them deep in the interior of the continent after the storm dissipates. So although bird-watchers never hope for destructive storms, we pay attention when tropical systems come ashore, knowing they might bring surprising birds to our local ponds.

Fast-Flying and Fierce

Fun facts on the lives of falcons, a group of fascinating predatory birds.

White morph gyrfalcon

10 Prairie falcons search for prey while soaring or peering from tall perches, but they also go on "strafing" flights as low as 10 feet off the ground as they look for food.

4 With a wingspan of 4 feet, the gyrfalcon (pronounced "JER-falcon") is the largest falcon. Your best bet to see this giant? Take a trip to Alaska or the Canadian tundra.

1986 Aplomado falcons have been listed as endangered since 1986. They're still very rare, but 1,500 released birds have boosted the population in the southern states.

2.8 The American kestrel is the smallest falcon. It weighs only 2.8 to 5.8 ounces, and it's small enough that a strong wind gust can knock it off course.

7 Seven falcon species are found in the U.S. and Canada. Two of them, gyrfalcons and aplomado falcons, are incredibly difficult to spot because of their range and scarcity.

American kestrel

1,300 Peregrine falcons lay their eggs on flat ledges or look for abandoned nests on cliff faces or tall structures. Their homes may be as low as 25 feet or as high as 1,300 feet, which is about the height of the Empire State Building in New York.

200 The peregrine falcon is the fastest animal on earth, flying up to 69 mph. That number is impressive, but it earned the title by its ability to dive after prey at speeds of over 200 mph.

Attracting Birds

Keep your feeders full of seasonal foods year-round—and the birds will keep coming back for more.

CHAPTER 4

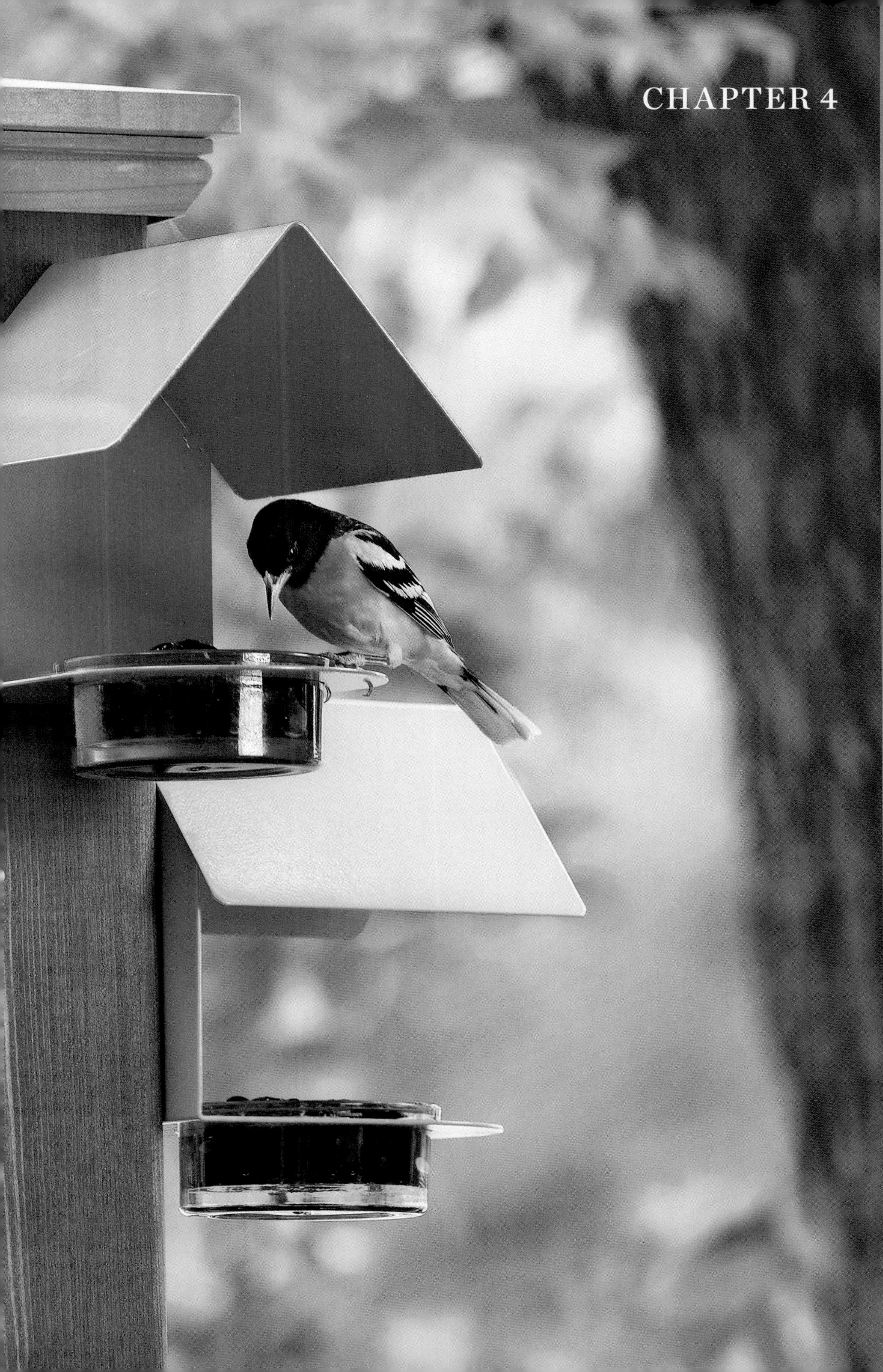

A clean feeder and fresh sugar water will make ruby-throated hummingbirds regular visitors.

How to Host a Feeding Frenzy

Maximize backyard traffic with tried-and-true tips from the pros.

A BIRD FEEDER is like a window to the natural world. It gives you a chance to delight in the antics and beauty of birds for hours of joy and learning. Best of all, feeding backyard fliers is simple—anyone can do it. Follow these tips to make the experience even better for you and for the birds.

Easy-to-serve and inexpensive grape jelly is the best way to lure Baltimore and other oriole species.

Keep Up with Cleaning

A clean feeder is essential, and it's definitely something to keep in mind when buying or building a new one. In addition to how attractive it looks, how sturdy it is and how much seed it holds, consider how easy it will be to clean a particular feeder. And then it's important to follow up by cleaning them thoroughly—once every few weeks for seed or suet feeders, once every few days for hummingbird feeders, and even more often in hot and humid weather.

Skip the Red Dye

Experts agree that red dye in hummingbird food is not only unnecessary, it could actually harm hummingbirds. The safest, most inexpensive way to provide hummingbird food (aside from adding native plants) is making your own: Stir four parts water with one part pure cane sugar. Bring to a boil, cool completely and fill your feeders.

Downy (top) and hairy woodpeckers nab a fatty meal from a suet feeder.

Male and female painted buntings stop to fill up at a millet feeder.

Go Beyond Seed

Bird feeding is rewarding even if you offer only one or two kinds of food. But adding variety to the menu attracts more kinds of birds. Black oil sunflower, thistle or Nyjer seed, and white millet are three of the staples. Add oranges and apples to attract orioles and catbirds, suet to lure woodpeckers, and peanuts to entice titmice, chickadees and nuthatches.

Say No to Grease

If you put up feeders, you may attract other "guests" to your yard. It's a challenge to keep squirrels from gobbling up expensive bird seed. You'll find a variety of baffles on the market, from simple to elaborate. Because squirrels are crafty little critters, you might need to try several to find the right device to baffle your marauder. But steer clear of grease or oil on hooks, poles or posts. Any oily substance can be fatal to birds if they get it on their feathers.

Remember: Location, Location, Location

Windows reflect outdoor scenery, so they pose a real danger to birds. You may have experienced that awful feeling when you hear a bird crash into a window. If this is a problem at your house, do whatever you can to reduce window strikes. Hawk silhouettes on the glass may help, or try using a product from American Bird Conservancy called BirdTape. It breaks up light and reflections so birds don't attempt to fly through. It is also easy to install and relatively inexpensive.

The position of the feeders makes a huge difference. The best place for one is either more than 5 feet from a large window or right next to it. When a feeder is farther away, the birds leaving it are less likely to fly into the glass; if the feeder is much closer, birds won't be flying at full speed if they happen to bump into the window.

A red-bellied woodpecker perches on a peanut feeder.

Don't Let the Cat Out

Feral cats and roaming house cats kill a billion birds each year. Although people often say that's just nature, it's not true; cats are not native here. Bird feeders and wandering cats are a recipe for disaster. Keeping cats indoors is better for native wildlife and for the cats, too. Let your cats do all their birding from indoors! If cats roam your neighborhood, either don't put out feeders or be sure to position them away from spots where the cats might lurk in ambush.

Offer Water Year-Round

Many songbirds stop over at feeders, but if you want to attract types that don't eat seeds—like warblers, vireos or thrushes—plan on making water a part of your feeding routine. So many kinds of birdbaths are available that it can be tough to choose, but the most natural location for a birdbath is on the ground. Make sure the basin isn't too deep. If your birdbath is more than 2 inches deep, add a layer of pea gravel to the bottom.

Birdbaths should just be shallow enough for birds to stand up. This basin is perfect for young eastern bluebirds.

Enjoy Your Visitors

Keeping feeders clean and full may feel like a big chore at times, so make sure to reward yourself by actually watching the birds at your feeders. Their behaviors are endlessly varied. Even people who've fed birds for decades can learn new things about their feathered visitors.

Branch Out

Make a natural perch. A dead branch with lots of little limbs is an attractive place to hang bird feeders. Simply wire the branch to a metal T-post or wooden pole to create a more natural look at your feeding station. Birds love to perch on the limbs, and the branches also provide a more natural setting for photography.

Share the Joy

One of the easiest ways to bring happiness to people's lives is to share your love of birds. Point out backyard birds to guests—or better yet, help friends and family with their own setup. A feeder and a bag of seed is a wonderful gift that keeps on giving for years, sparking a lifelong hobby.

Orange halves are attractive to many birds, including orioles, catbirds and this scarlet tanager.

As the weather heats up, lure young families by focusing less on serving seeds and more on special foods such as mealworms.

Summer Switch-Up

Find out why some people stop feeding the birds when warm weather arrives.

BACKYARD FEEDERS OFFER A FOOD SOURCE FOR neighborhood birds when wild pickings are scarce, especially in winter. Birds could get by in any season without your offerings, no doubt, but it's clear they enjoy the sunflower seed buffets. During the summer months, however, when bugs and plants are prevalent, many wonder: *Should I be feeding the birds?* The short answer is that it's perfectly fine to feed birds year-round, with proper care.

Warm temperatures lead to an increase in infectious diseases. When wildlife (say, birds eating at feeders) come together in close proximity, the spread of disease is more likely. Summer heat can cause seed and suet to spoil or become moldy much quicker, especially if your feeders are in the sun.

Research shows that feeding in summer may have an upside. A study in the journal *Conservation Physiology* found that despite the fact that feeder birds had more diseases on average, those same birds were also in better physical condition than other wild birds. Travis Wilcoxen and his co-authors write, "Generally, the individual health of birds improved with supplemental feeding."

Like so many things in life, to feed or not to feed has no clear-cut answer. *Birds & Blooms* field editor Juli Seyfried of Cincinnati, Ohio, sets out suet and mixed seeds in winter, but says, "Come spring, we stop feeding because insects are available."

But many bird-watchers do set out seed feeders in summer because of certain seasonal perks. "Birds bring their fledglings to the yard when they know there's a reliable food source," says Jen St. Louis of Elmira, Ontario. "I love watching the babies flap about and beg their parents to feed them. They're too cute!"

If you are eager to feed during the summer—because seeing the colorful, seasonal birds up close is a real joy—then it's important that you keep your feeders and surrounding areas clean to avoid spreading illness. Spray and wipe feeders with a 10% bleach solution, rinse well and dry. Do this every few fillings. Once or twice per season, take them down and give them a full wash with hot water and soap, or run them through the dishwasher. Also be sure to sweep up the husks and dropped seeds.

If you don't want to keep feeders up or can't keep them clean during the summer months, the birds will still be fine without you. When the cool weather of fall comes in, refill the feeders in time to watch the autumn migrants and winter resident species return!

SUMMER MENU
Add variety to your offerings as the seasons change. Summer favorites include oranges for orioles, mealworms for bluebirds and sugar water for hummingbirds.

"We feed the birds year-round, however, we have to pay close attention that other critters aren't getting at the food, especially deer!"

Patrick Hogan
TEMPERANCE, MICHIGAN

HOT-WEATHER HABITS
Fill your feeders halfway in summer, so the food is less likely to go bad and won't go to waste. Once the seed or suet has spoiled, toss it out.

Ground-Level Buffets

Attract towhees, juncos, sparrows and more by serving food on all available flat surfaces.

MANY SPECIES FLY RIGHT BY FEEDERS, choosing to forage for food on the ground instead. The easiest way to entice these birds, says Nancy Castillo, a co-owner of the Wild Birds Unlimited store in Saratoga Springs, New York, is to "sprinkle small amounts of seed, especially around shrubs, to attract birds that prefer eating on the ground, like towhees, juncos and native sparrows." Some larger birds, including thrashers, quails, doves and cardinals, also prefer to dig into flat-surface spreads.

Go Easy on the Seeds

Sunflower and safflower seeds, cracked corn and seed blends are all fine for sprinkling directly on the ground. It's best to serve only a little each day as opposed to piling up a bunch of seeds. This protects seeds from soggy weather and reduces overnight visitors to the feeding area. Nancy recommends a no-mess blend of white millet and sunflower seeds. "That way everything gets eaten," she says. "This strategy might also attract birds that cannot open seed shells, like wrens, catbirds and warblers."

Serve Near Shelter

Birds known for their skulking nature rarely stray far from cover, so as you landscape, remember your ground-feeding friends. By providing shelter, you give birds security while they feed. They can quickly retreat to a thicket if an aerial predator like a Cooper's hawk swoops by. Sprinkling seeds along hedgerows is another safe option. Focusing on the leeward side also protects birds and seeds from the elements.

Elevate the Offerings

It's possible to coax ground-feeding birds to feeders. "A tray feeder with excellent drainage is another way to cater to these birds," Nancy says. Seed trays, platforms and shelf feeders bring the seeds off the ground while maintaining the large, flat surface area many birds prefer. Another option is to fill an empty birdbath with seeds. When coupled with baffles, feeders help to deter raccoons, opossums and other critters looking for a meal.

Cleanup Required

One main benefit of spreading seeds on the ground is that you have the entire yard to work with. You can rotate the serving area throughout the seasons rather than concentrating on one spot. And with all types of bird feeding, it's very important to maintain cleanliness. Seed hulls can easily be raked up, while feeders should get a good scrubbing regularly. This cuts down on the growth of bacteria and fungi—and keeps unwanted guests away.

SUPER SEED EATERS

The common ground dove is a sparrow-sized species found in the southern tier of states from California to South Carolina. They nest and feed on the ground. It is estimated that a common ground dove consumes over 2,500 seeds in a single day, storing hundreds at a time in a two-lobed pocket near the esophagus called a crop.

"My feeder birds enjoy seeds sprinkled on the ground, too. When traffic is heavy, they'll feed around the post base."

Lori Bowers
CROSSVILLE, TENNESSEE

CLEANUP CREW

Dark-eyed juncos are among the most abundant species, with numbers estimated in the hundreds of millions. In much of their range, they appear in autumn and retreat north as spring arrives—often feeding on fallen seed.

Grow a Bird Buffet

When these flowers fade, seeds feed hungry songbirds.

1

PERFECT FOR POTS
Reaching more than 4 feet tall, Purple Majesty millet is an ideal specimen for the center of an autumn container combo.

1 Purple Majesty millet

PENNISETUM GLAUCUM, ANNUAL

Imagine a corn plant wearing a majestic deep purple robe. That's a great description of this 2003 All-America Selections winner (a well-deserved award!). Enjoy its graceful 4- to 5-foot stature all summer. Come fall, cut cattail-like seedpods for dried floral arrangements or leave them for the birds to snack on in winter.
Why we love it: It's easy to grow, drought tolerant and a focal piece alone or next to companions with contrasting foliage.

2 Cosmos

COSMOS BIPINNATUS, ANNUAL

This bright and classic garden annual is a perfect addition to troublesome bare patches in perennial beds. Simply spread some seed and let cosmos come back year after year—it easily self-seeds without becoming a pest. Some cultivars grow 2 to 4 feet, and feature white, pink, lavender and magenta flowers that bloom from June to frost.
Why we love it: With its ferny foliage, cosmos is attractive even when grown in dry, lean soils.

3 Marigold

TAGETES SPP., ANNUAL

You have to admire a plant that puts out a summer's worth of brightly colored yellow, orange, white or even bicolored blooms—and then keeps producing in fall until a hard frost. African marigolds (*T. erecta*), at up to 3 feet, are the tallest, while French marigolds (*T. patula*) grow just 6 to 18 inches tall but stall in heat.
Why we love it: Among the brightest flowers you'll find, marigolds are easy to deadhead and keep blooming. And they're easy to start from seed.

4 Autumn Joy sedum

SEDUM, ZONES 3 TO 9

This pretty 2-foot-tall succulent makes very few demands in terms of watering or fertilizing. Its only fault is splaying when there's too much shade or the soil is rich or wet, so shear the foliage back by about half in June, or plant in a different location.
Why we love it: Three seasons of interest—blue-gray summer foliage, rose pink to burgundy flowers in fall, and forms that are beautiful topped with a dusting of snow in winter.

5 Black-eyed Susan

RUDBECKIA SPP., ZONES 3 TO 10

Black-eyed Susan is a popular plant with a long season of blooms. It's full of bright, cheerful, daisylike flowers that lend a golden hue to the garden from midsummer to frost. Depending on species and cultivar, rudbeckia grow anywhere from 1 to 8 feet tall.

Why we love it: Some biennial types have pretty tri-tone marks. Try one to add some pizazz to your garden.

6 Coreopsis

COREOPSIS SPP., ZONES 3 TO 9

Coreopsis is known for its bright golden flowers—some bicolored in burgundy hues. But cultivars also come with pink and red blooms. Heights of popular species range from 6 inches to 3 feet. It's a long bloomer if deadheaded. To get more flowers, trim back after the first flush of flowers. Wait for it to rebloom later in summer, then let the second batch of flowers go to seed.

Why we love it: Adaptable and with dependable color, coreopsis selections can be grown as mounded ground covers or middle-of-the-border showpieces.

7 Goldenrod

SOLIDAGO SPP., ZONES 4 TO 9

Goldenrod is a traditional fall flower and a lovely addition to the garden when little else is in bloom. It grows from 18 inches to 4 feet or more, depending on species and cultivar. It's an excellent source of nectar for migrating pollinators and birds eat the seeds, so leave spent flowers in place.

Why we love it: Its long golden yellow flower clusters are deer resistant and grace gardens into early fall.

8 Purple coneflower

ECHINACEA PURPUREA, ZONES 3 TO 9

Coneflowers have a fresh look these days, thanks to new introductions with colors from yellow and white to tomato soup orange. Traditional types are best for feeding birds. This perennial peaks at just the right time—when summer heat has taken a toll on many other plants.

Why we love it: The large, showy flowers have prominent centers that stay on stems for winter interest.

9 Zinnia

ZINNIA ELEGANS, ANNUAL

With heights from 6 inches to 3 feet, there's a zinnia for every garden. And with such a range of colors—red, yellow, orange, chartreuse, pink, lavender, white—there's a zinnia for every taste as well. Use the smaller types as edging plants and larger varieties in the back of beds. Some can even work as barriers or privacy screens.

Why we love it: With zinnia seeds, you create a parade of colors that lasts all summer.

10 Sunflower

HELIANTHUS ANNUUS, ANNUAL

This fast-growing annual reaches 10 feet or more, so sow a handful of seeds and step back. New cultivars, just 1 to 2 feet tall, are ideal for pots. Sunflowers may be the best-known flower of summer, and birds love them. Wait until the flower heads dry and the seeds are mature to remove from your garden.

Why we love it: Crazy simple to germinate, it reaches impressive heights—and those seeds!

Small Space Sanctuaries

Easy ways to welcome feathered friends to a yard of any size.

YOUR FAVORITE BACKYARD FLIERS aren't picky about the size of your garden. They are far more interested in the food and shelter you offer. Whether you're working with square acres or square feet, use small space gardening strategies to create your best bird oasis.

Melinda Myers, *Birds & Blooms'* resident gardening expert and author of *Small Space Gardening*, is well-versed in designing for compact areas, and skillfully transformed her own small city lot. Her best advice: "Start with a plan. This is even more important with small yards since you have limited space to accomplish your goal of creating an attractive area for you and the wildlife you are trying to invite in."

Focus on the Basics

Melinda adds, "Just like us, animals need food, shelter, water and a place to raise their young. If you focus on these essentials, they'll come to your landscape."

Make every square inch count with compact plants that thrive in your growing conditions, are native to your area, offer seeds or berries, and provide a place for birds to nest.

"Include some seed-producing plants like coneflower. Allow them to set seed, along with annuals like cosmos and salvia, and watch the birds come to dine," Melinda says.

Pentas, cuphea, phlox, lantana, zinnia, ageratum, and dill and other herbs are also ideal for attracting wildlife, she says. If you are looking to draw in more pollinators and butterflies but

Some birds skip feeders but are drawn to water. Adding a small birdbath is a space-saving way to attract them.

Flat-backed hanging grow bags filled with petunias are attractive and draw in pollinators, like bees and hummingbirds.

Common yellowthroat on a sunflower

serviceberry because it grows narrow and upright, and is packed with ornamental fruit for birds. Grasses such as switch grasses or prairie dropseed also offer major wildlife benefits and provide lovely texture.

Before you check out at the garden center, read the plant tags thoroughly. Young plants may be labeled as dwarf, or just look small, but have the potential to outgrow your space quickly and make it feel even smaller.

Sculpt Your Space

Once you pick the plants, it's time to set them in place. Instead of visualizing your yard as a flat expanse, imagine it as a set of layers and slowly work your way up.

Start with ground cover and mix annuals and perennials, placing shorter plants in front. Melinda suggests doubling up plantings for continued interest through the seasons.

"Place bulbs among perennials. The early flowering bulbs add needed color for us and a source of nectar for pollinators. And as the bulbs fade and foliage declines, the perennials emerge, masking any unsightly foliage and adding more flowers," she explains.

When you run out of room, start thinking about containers. They're a fabulous way to add growth and color to otherwise unworkable areas, such as concrete patios or walkways.

don't have lots of space, swamp milkweed and butterfly weed are more contained than common milkweed and are excellent nectar sources.

Melinda suggests growing a diverse set of native plants to support pollinators and the health and beauty of your yard. Some plants mature and spread faster than others and throw off the variety in small lots. To save yourself some work, find plants that do not reseed easily and make sure to manage new growth.

It may seem like a lot to ask, but even small yards need trees or shrubs for the height, structure and shelter they provide to wildlife. Many dwarf evergreens fit the bill, or consider a serviceberry. Melinda favors the obelisk

White-breasted
nuthatches are
happy to eat from
compact trays.

To feel safe, birds prefer a space with cover. Shrubs and hanging baskets offer shelter in this garden.

From miniature evergreens to vines, you'd be surprised which plants thrive in pots. Just be sure the container is large enough to hold it.

When you've completely exhausted space on the ground, remember: The sky is the limit. Features like trellises, window boxes, vertical pallet containers, flat-backed hanging planters or even a tabletop pot give gardens a finished look and make your yard feel more private.

Finally, set up feeders and a small birdbath, and give yourself some space to enjoy the fruits of your hard work. "Make sure you have a good view of your new features, including visiting birds and butterflies," Melinda says. "A bench or chair to sit back and enjoy a spring evening makes all the difference."

COMMUNITY LIVING

Four ways to draw winged visitors to an apartment balcony or patio.

1. Focus on containers. Many perennials and annuals that attract wildlife in larger yards are well suited for small planters and pots.

2. Plant particular flowers that offer multiple benefits, like alliums, black-eyed Susans, marigolds and sunflowers, near a window for prime viewing.

3. Add vertical interest and entice pollinators with cardinal vines, honeysuckle vines and climbing nasturtiums.

4. Set out bird feeders and a small birdbath, be patient, and appreciate all visitors, whether they are avian or insect.

What's your best tip for feeding winter birds?

Attract more cold-weather warriors with knowledgeable reader advice.

For winter feeding, I buy a 50-pound bag of chicken scratch feed and a 25-pound bag of black sunflower seed from the local co-op. I mix them together in a large container with a tight lid. It creates a quality mix for less than $25!

Tom Baldwin HATFIELD, ARKANSAS

Serve sunflower and thistle seeds and high-energy suet cakes.

Rodney Blackwell FOREST CITY, ILLINOIS

Leave seed-bearing flowers in the garden instead of cutting them back in fall.

Judy Roberts GRAYTOWN, OHIO

Anna's hummingbird

Red-headed woodpeckers

Hang feeders in a place you can easily access. It's so easy to refill them often when you don't have to walk through snow or ice.

Joann Sklarsky JOHNSTOWN, PENNSYLVANIA

Hummingbirds visit year-round, so when the temps are below freezing I hang a cluster of Christmas tree lights under my feeders. It provides enough heat to keep them from freezing.

Sharon Mayhew
VANCOUVER, WASHINGTON

I fill an old birdbath with seed. It attracts a lot of ground-feeding birds that typically stay away from feeders. It also keeps the sparrows from hogging your feeder.

Liza Peniston AUGUSTA, KANSAS

CHAPTER 5

Garden Know-How

Use tried-and-true planting tips and top flower suggestions to beautify your landscape.

Growing Trends

Explore the latest and greatest ideas and practices on the garden scene.

EVERY NEW GROWING SEASON brings a fresh wave of garden trends. Some are brand-new while others are timeless ideas that never go out of style. Always a popular hobby, gardening continues to gain traction as new generations see its health and relaxation benefits and jump on the bandwagon. Watch your local garden center for signs that these greener ways are on the rise.

Bringing the Outdoors In

Plants continue to move indoors in a big way. It's nearly impossible to look at a magazine spread or watch a home decor show without seeing a live fiddle-leaf fig, succulent or other kind of greenery used as key design elements.

Millennials and many others are quickly discovering the power of plants to help combat stress, connect with nature and purify the air. Research validates the environmental and health benefits of living with plants—blood pressure and stress levels drop while mood improves. NASA also verified that many plants improved indoor air quality by removing toxins linked to sick building syndrome.

Downsizing baby boomers are joining millennials in embracing the indoor plant craze. Houseplants allow gardening to continue even with limited outdoor space. Those who were growing houseplants in the '70s will find that terrariums and macrame are back in style.

Using indoor plants to purify the air and add funky shapes is on the rise among people of all ages.

LEFT: Grow plants, like this calendula, that benefit pollinators. BELOW: Use pots to add leafy hostas to patios and balconies. RIGHT: Make veggie gardening a family affair—get your kids and grandchildren involved, too!

Planting for Pollinators

Beneficial bugs remain a top concern for gardeners and environmentalists alike. The decline of honeybees and monarchs created public awareness of the importance of all pollinators. One out of three foods we eat depends on the work of insects. Knowing this, hundreds of thousands of gardeners, schools and cities are joining programs and registering their gardens, landscapes and other green spaces as pollinator- and wildlife-friendly areas.

Focusing on growing more native plants and eliminating the use of harmful chemicals are just two ways gardeners improve their landscape's pollinator appeal. Even a small container garden on a balcony makes a difference. Adopting a more casual approach to gardening is an easy step to take. Leave a layer of leaves on the ground for the bumblebees, and let perennials stand through the cold months to provide winter homes for beneficial insects and food for the birds.

Take the level of commitment up a notch by registering your garden in the Million Pollinator Garden Challenge of the National Pollinator Garden Network. Check with the National Wildlife Federation to see if your yard qualifies as a Certified Backyard Wildlife Habitat.

Growing Good Food

More people are growing a portion of their family's food. Some are motivated by the flavor and nutrition that fresh produce brings, while others are more concerned about the safety of store-bought food. With homegrown herbs, fruits and vegetables, you control what is applied to the plants and shorten the time from harvest to your dinner table. Grow it and you are more likely to eat it, no matter your age or past reluctance to eat vegetables. Another bonus: Scientists have discovered an antidepressant soil microbe and are studying how it helps fight a variety of diseases and disorders. Dirt is good for you!

You don't need a big space or even the outdoors. New compact vegetable varieties with colorful foliage, fruits and flowers fit into any pot, container garden or small bed, and improved energy-efficient lights and hydroponic systems allow people to grow more edibles indoors. It's possible to harvest radishes, lettuce, microgreens, herbs, and even tomatoes and other vegetables from an indoor garden.

Tomatoes can be grown indoors!

Potting Up Style

Interest in container gardens is still on the upswing. Urban dwellers create inviting spaces with pots, elevated gardens and rail planters filled with flowers and edibles. People with limited time or physical restrictions find container gardening less demanding.

No matter the size of your landscape, containers bring the garden to anyone's door. Containers of flowers create living centerpieces while pots filled with herbs and veggies add homegrown flavor to meals.

Creating a Great Escape

Whether it's a backyard or local public green space, more people are turning to nature. The forest bathing trend encourages people to go on a slow stroll through a woodland to soak in the sights and sounds. Mindful walks in nature have been shown to help reduce blood pressure and stress while increasing focus and energy.

You don't have to go to the woods to sooth your senses. Sales of essential oils used in aromatherapy are increasing rapidly. Gardeners are also growing more herbs for fragrance or as herbal teas and body treatments. For example, peppermint aids digestion, fights inflammation and increases alertness. You can grow nature's sweetener, stevia, and munch on a leaf to stave off that sugar craving or use it to sweeten a favorite drink or dish. Then relax away the stress of the day with the help of lavender herb or oil.

Go Native

Learn the benefits of adding these valuable plants to your landscape.

Native flowering dogwood and other spring-blooming trees offer shelter to migrating birds like this prothonotary warbler.

THE EFFORT TO GROW NATIVES IS WORTH IT. These beauties improve the environment in so many ways because they've evolved over time with the birds, bees and animals that depend on them. Natives are attractive, remove impurities from the air, release oxygen, and help manage stormwater, reducing the risk of flooding. Their deep roots create pathways for rainwater to move through the soil instead of running off into streets, and they filter out contaminants in the water before it returns to groundwater sources.

Gulf fritillary butterfly on blanket flower

EXPAND YOUR SEARCH

Native plants are plentiful and diverse. Contact your local nature center, botanical garden or extension office for guidance. Blanket flower (1), purple coneflower (2), bee balm (3) and coreopsis (4) are a few of the best options.

It's worthwhile—and easy—to work natives into your current landscape. No matter the size of your garden, patio, balcony or window box, natives fit in anywhere.

Make the Switch

Starting slowly is often the key to long-term success. Look for ways to easily add local plants to existing beds and containers. Fill empty spaces or replace struggling greenery with a native tree, shrub or perennial suited to the growing conditions and decorative needs of your garden. Or dedicate an entire section to natives. Organize in masses or small clusters for the greatest visual impact. Group the plants in a way that allows winged visitors to gather food more efficiently.

Another option is to dedicate an entire section to an all-natural plot. Leave a strip of mown grass or decorative fencing around the perimeter and add a birdhouse or feeder to signal to neighbors that you are gardening with a purpose. But before you start, contact your local municipality for

any regulations related to growing this type of landscape in your neighborhood.

Prepare the soil before putting your plants in the ground. Because most backyard soils were altered during the building of homes and communities, give the soil a boost with compost or other organic matter. Work it into the top 12 inches of soil and rake smooth before planting your natives.

For the first few years, you may need to provide a bit of TLC and weed control, but once established, native perennials flourish and bloom with minimal care. Many are quite vigorous and quickly fill a small urban or suburban lot. Choose plants carefully, combine those that are equally assertive, and do a bit of regular dividing if you need to control their enthusiastic spread.

Bird Magnets

Soon, you'll start to see one of the major benefits of growing native. The plants feed your favorite birds for free! Hummingbirds visit to sip nectar

species that produce seeds and berries during different seasons to provide a steady source of food.

Drawing birds in with native plants has advantages beyond feeding. During the growing season, many nesting songbirds and hummingbirds feed on insects and, consequently, help manage pests in your garden. And native plants provide shelter for birds and other critters that live or pass through your neighborhood.

Pollinator-Friendly

Native plants offer benefits to all kinds of fliers. Butterflies, native bees and other pollinators are critical to the food we eat and natural beauty we enjoy. By cultivating a habitat where they thrive, you help them produce the next generation of plants. Butterflies nectar on a variety of indigenous flowers, and caterpillars depend on natives as a food source. Most flowering plants need an animal, usually an insect, to visit them in search of food, transporting pollen from flower to flower so they can produce seeds. It's a win-win for all.

Once the native spaces are well established, leave your yard in a more natural state. Many bugs make their homes in the hollow stems of perennials and shrubs, debris piles and tree cavities. Letting perennials stand in winter and leaving leaf litter on the ground is a simple way to increase the population of wildlife, native bees and beneficial bugs.

As you experience and share the benefits and beauty of growing natives, you might even find you have started an eco-friendly trend in your own neighborhood!

from honeysuckle vine or columbine, and songbirds dine on the seeds of coneflowers, black-eyed Susans and sunflowers. Leaving seed-producing perennials in place for winter is a super simple way to supplement the bird feeders in your yard.

Go one step further and expand your offerings to include native berry-producing shrubs and trees like dogwood, viburnum, serviceberry and holly. Growing a variety of local plants helps attract birds year-round. Be sure to look for tree

NATIVE PICKS

Find your region, and get growing these local gems.

EAST OF THE ROCKIES

Columbine
Woodland phlox
Common milkweed
Bee balm
Purple coneflower
Aster

FLORIDA

Red columbine
Coreopsis
Gaillardia
Swamp lily
Swamp mallow
Sandhill milkweed

ROCKY MOUNTAINS

Columbine
Showy milkweed
Scarlet gilia
Fireweed
Mountain lupine
Western wallflower

SOUTHWEST

California poppy
Yellow columbine
Showy milkweed
Autumn sage
Pineleaf penstemon
Texas red yucca

PACIFIC NORTHWEST

Western columbine
Lewisia
Goatsbeard
Wild hollyhock
Western lily
Wetland aster

Multiply Your Plants

Follow these steps to produce more of your top picks for free.

Lantana is an easy plant to clone using the stem cutting process.

Rooted lavender plants are almost ready to be transplanted into the garden.

1. SNIP off a 4- to 6-inch section of new growth, cutting immediately above a node, the swollen area where a leaf forms, and trim the cutting stem so a node is close to the base. Take cuttings early in the morning when the plant tissues have the most moisture.

2. REMOVE leaves from the bottom half of the stem. This reduces moisture loss while leaving some foliage for photosynthesis.

3. COAT the base of the stem in rooting hormone to help stimulate root growth and reduce rot.

4. INSERT the bottom inch of stem with the rooting hormone into a premoistened mix of half peat moss and half vermiculite. Firmly tamp soil around the stem.

5. MIST stem and leaves with a spray of water, then loosely place a clear plastic bag over the plant to increase humidity.

6. PLACE the covered plant 6 inches below a fluorescent light. Remove the plastic cover and transplant when roots are coming out of the drainage holes or pressing against the sides of the container.

TO SAVE MONEY, try rooting stem cuttings. It's simple—find a straight species, an older cultivar or plant not under a patent, clip off a juvenile section of the plant's stem, then coax roots to grow from it. Just think, you can clone as many examples of the mother plant as you wish for the cost of potting medium and a jar of rooting hormone.

"Because many plants root readily from cuttings, this is one of the most popular forms of propagation, especially for trees, shrubs and vines," says Justin Hancock, horticulturist at Costa Farms. "Propagating with cuttings doesn't usually interfere with the plants' growth, and you don't need to worry about pollinating a flower and waiting for the seeds to ripen—or digging up the plant to take root cuttings."

Stem cuttings can be taken in spring, summer or fall, depending on the plant species. Pliable spring cuttings are called softwood cuttings. Semi-hardwood cuttings are a little more rigid and are gathered in late summer. Finally, hardwood cuttings are taken when plants are dormant in late fall or winter, stored for the cold months, then rooted the following spring.

The benefits of rooting cuttings versus starting from seed? "It gives you an exact clone of the one you propagated from," Justin says. "Seeds, because they're a combination of the mother and father plants' DNA, usually provide some variation." Depending on the species, stem cuttings also give you a bigger plant, faster.

IDEAL FOR CUTTING

- Abelia
- Beauty bush (*Kolkwitzia*)
- Bittersweet (*Celastrus*)
- Cassiope
- Chaste tree (*Vitex*)
- Chocolate vine (*Akebia*)
- Cotoneaster
- Crape myrtle (*Lagerstroemia*)
- Deutzia
- Flowering quince (*Chaenomeles*)
- Fothergilla
- Lantana
- Lavender
- Madagascar dragon tree (*Dracaena marginata*)
- Plumbago
- Serviceberry (*Amelanchier*)
- Smokebush (*Cotinus*)
- St. John's wort (*Hypericum*)
- Summersweet (*Clethra*)
- Viburnum
- Virginia sweetspire (*Itea*)
- Witch hazel (*Hamamelis*)

Container Stars

Freshen up your pots with late-summer bloomers.

1

Infinity Pink New Guinea impatiens

1 Petunia

PETUNIA, ANNUAL

This heat-loving annual produces trumpet-shaped blooms well into fall with a little TLC. Coax more color from the plant by pinching off the seedpods and removing dead, faded flowers. With enough sun and water, petunias will keep blooming until the first hard freeze.

Why we love it: Flowers come in almost every color, and some even bring their own contrast with bicolored blooms.

2 Impatiens

IMPATIENS, ANNUAL

No wonder impatiens are a mainstay in shade gardens, where color can be tough to come by. Keep them well-watered and fed, and they'll reward you with nonstop blooms. With so many cultivars available, you're sure to find a variety that piques your fancy.

Why we love it: These beauties are naturally self-cleaning, meaning they drop their faded blooms so you don't have to deadhead.

3 Cosmos

COSMOS, ANNUAL

These self-seeders do particularly well in lean soil, and some shorter varieties thrive in containers. They grow 2 to 4 feet tall and are available in a range of colors, including pink, purple, white, yellow, orange and red. Plant just before the last spring frost.

Why we love it: The lacy foliage is a delight to behold, and once the flowers appear, bees are sure to follow.

4 Aster

ASTER OR *SYMPHYOTRICHUM*, ZONES 3 TO 8

Just as early and midsummer bloomers begin to fade, asters burst into color and give your garden another wave of bright pigment. The daisylike flowers come in many colors including blue, pink, purple, red and white. Be sure to pick a variety that's small enough to fit in your container and pinch it back regularly.

Why we love it: Asters provide a steady supply of nectar for late-season butterflies and bees.

Toucan Yellow
canna

5 Marigold

TAGETES, ANNUAL

One of the easiest bedding annuals to propagate and grow, all sunny marigold needs is a little water and an occasional sprinkle of fertilizer. Flowering may slow down a bit during the middle of summer, but deadhead to keep these colorful stalwarts blooming until the first hard freeze. **Why we love it:** Marigolds keep giving. Let a few flowers go to seed in the fall for a new batch of blooms next year.

6 Canna

CANNA, ZONES 7 TO 10

While canna's flower spikes are impressive in their own right, the plant is beloved for its foliage. Its large, extremely bold leaves create a tropical effect when combined with other bright, flowering plants. It's best grown in a sunny spot with moist, well-draining soil.
Why we love it: Canna grows from fleshy rhizomes that can be dug up in fall and overwintered in sawdust or peat moss in a cool, dry area. Replant the rhizomes next spring, after the threat of frost passes.

7 Celosia

CELOSIA ARGENTEA, ANNUAL

Sometimes called cockscomb, celosia holds its color even in the dog days of summer. Plants grow from 6 inches to 3 feet tall and feature either green or bronze foliage. Look for varieties with orange, red, purple, yellow or cream crested flower heads.
Why we love it: With their compact spread, these showy blooms add height and an explosion of color to any summer container. They also do well in dry soil.

Dahlightful Tupelo Honey dahlia

8 Dusty miller

JACOBAEA MARTIMA, ZONES 7 TO 10 OR ANNUAL

The silver, fuzzy foliage of dusty miller, also called silver ragwort, makes a fine companion for tall, colorful plants. It's best kept in full sun to part shade, where it will keep its unique metallic hues. At maturity, the plant forms a rounded 6- to 15-inch clump.

Why we love it: Along with being an ideal costar, dusty miller is also low maintenance and is able to grow in rocky soil.

9 Dahlia

DAHLIA SPP., ZONES 7 TO 10 OR ANNUAL

Dahlias hit their stride in late summer. The many hybrids are organized into 14 different groups, and come in such a wide range of flower colors and plant heights you'll find one to suit almost any pot. Deadhead blooms until frost for more color.

Why we love it: Where winters are cold, dig up the tubers after a killing frost and store them in a cool, dry area. Then replant in spring.

10 Nasturtium

TROPAEOLUM, ZONES 2 TO 11

Tough and wiry nasturtium is a reliable source of orange, red and yellow hues. It really looks great spilling from containers but grows vertically with the right cultivar and support. This garden classic also takes poor or rocky soil in stride.

Why we love it: If the peppery, edible flowers aren't exciting enough, the bright green, rounded leaves with intriguing markings ought to do it.

Succulent Obsessed

Everything you need to know about the stylish, low-maintenance plants you set and forget.

Echeverias like this one require minimal care and are diverse in color and shape.

Left: Hummelii sedeveria's versatile red tips shine in indoor containers or thrive as annuals in outdoor beds.

THE INFATUATION WITH SUCCULENTS started simply enough. Their tendency to thrive on inattention plus strong geometric shapes captured the attention of many gardeners. Now the tough-as-nails plants are more popular than ever.

These drought-resistant, perfectly plump plants are both easy to care for and offer tons of flair. The range of colors—blue-green, lime, yellow, red, burgundy and more—is matched only by the fascinating variety of leaf shapes, including rounded, ruffled, spiky and needlelike choices.

"They're so textural and many plants have distinctive, unique looks, and that helped to propel succulents as 'it' plants," explains Justin Hancock of Costa Farms, one of the world's largest succulent and houseplant growers.

With so many looks, there's bound to be a succulent you fancy, whether it's an upright African milk tree, low-mounding echeveria, or trailing elephant bush. Many make excellent indoor plants, preferring

the dry, warm air typically found in homes.

Succulents are excellent options for gardeners who love containers but don't like the idea of watering them every day. They shine by themselves or with companions like snake plant, ZZ plant and ponytail palm.

"They are a natural fit for container gardens, especially in hot, sunny spots that tend to dry out fast," says Justin. "Low-growing varieties are fantastic as edging plants or in mass plantings for a look that doesn't require a lot of care."

Happily, there are both tender and hardy succulents, so you can enjoy them in many different ways. In general, they just need a few consistent conditions.

"Bright light and well-draining potting mix or soil are a must," Justin says. "Even though they're touted as easy-care plants, most succulents will fail if their roots stay wet or they don't get enough bright light."

Insert a toothpick into the drainage holes at the bottom of

the pot to gauge how much water is in the soil. "If it comes out clean, the mix is dry and you should water your succulent," says Justin. "If bits of potting mix are adhering to it, then there's enough moisture and you probably don't need to water just yet."

Succulents grow slower than other plants—some don't noticeably grow for months—so they don't require much fertilizer. Feed them as infrequently as once or twice a year in spring or summer, or push them to grow faster by fertilizing every time you water. Just be sure to follow application rates on the fertilizer label.

WHAT TO GROW

Choose low-maintenance stunners from thousands of succulent options.

1 DESERT ROSE looks like a bonsai, so it's a perfect pick for creating textural contrast.

2 SUNSPARKLER BLUE ELF SEDUM is hardy, coming back every year in most regions, with blue-gray foliage and pink flowers.

3 HAWORTHIA FASCIATA, with dark green leaves and crisp white bands, is among the toughest succulents.

4 FANTASTIC KALANCHOE features green, paddlelike leaves edged with colorful cream, pink, red and purple streaks.

5 CAMPFIRE CRASSULA, with its rich green foliage, takes on bright orange and red tones in cool weather.

In the Limelight

Blooms in chartreuse hues steal the show in any garden.

1

1 Green Star gladiola

GLADIOLUS, ZONES 8 TO 11

This rising star is ideal for adding tiers of height to your garden. About 10 to 12 of the 3-inch florets along the stem open all at once during their July and August performances. Butterflies are also big fans. Grow Green Star near burgundy, purple or white blooms.

Why we love it: Reaching 4 feet tall, these pastel giants add drama to summer bouquets.

2 Envy zinnia

ZINNIA, ANNUAL

It's not the color of these nearly 3-inch double and semidouble chartreuse blooms that evokes garden envy—it's how easy zinnias are to grow. They grow quickly from seed, pop with color all summer long and make lovely cut flowers. And their 2-foot height shades out weeds.

Why we love it: In addition to all the pros of zinnias, they happen to be hummingbird and butterfly magnets.

3 Little Lime hydrangea

HYDRANGEA PANICULATA, ZONES 4 TO 8

Little Lime is a dwarf version of the popular Limelight hydrangea, but it still puts on a big show. Growing between 3 and 5 feet, it makes an attractive border for smaller spaces. Sturdy stems mean this smaller specimen knows how to hold its head up high, refusing to be overshadowed.

Why we love it: Although gorgeous in pale green, it's pretty in pink in the late summer, as it begins to blush when fall is in the air.

4 Green Gambler hellebore

HELLEBORUS, ZONES 4 TO 9

As part of the Winter Thriller series of Lenten rose, the Green Gambler is a sure bet, paying off in long-lasting green flowers. Look for cultivars featuring a burgundy wine silhouette for even more interest. Typically flowering in their second year when starting from seed, plants grow 18 to 24 inches tall and flower just when you need them most: winter. Plant in partial or full shade for best results.

Why we love it: It's an early bloomer, showing its petals in early spring. Perhaps with a little luck, you'll have green blooms for St. Patrick's Day.

5 Lime Green flowering tobacco

NICOTIANA ALATA, ANNUAL

This sun-loving plant has a pleasant aroma and an even more pleasant appearance. Growing about 3 feet high and nearly 2 feet across, it makes your garden glow with 1½-inch starry flowers that bloom from sunny summer right into autumn.

Why we love it: Flowering tobacco smells sweeter by evening and into the night, making your star-studded garden even more dreamy.

6 Sophistica Lime Green petunia

PETUNIA X HYBRIDA, ANNUAL

Petunias are perhaps the most popular annuals, but the lime green ones add a special rarity and striking contrast to hanging baskets and potted arrangements. This designer seed produces large 3½-inch flowers with somewhat star-shaped blooms, growing about 10 to 15 inches high and unfurling to an impressive 10 to 12 inches wide.

Why we love it: Petunias tolerate heat and forgetful gardeners, requiring watering only about once a week (but try to check containers daily).

7 Bells of Ireland

MOLUCCELLA LAEVIS, ANNUAL

These so-called Irish beauties will have your garden ringing with the green. It's the bell shape that keeps them true to their name. They feature tiny fragrant white flowers that grow in large green calyxes (the protective layers around the petals). The result is striking bloom spikes that bring your garden to new heights from July to September. They perform best in cool weather. Plant in full sun for best results.

Why we love it: If you're fluent in the language of flowers, then you know that Bells of Ireland are a symbol of good luck.

8 Evergreen amaryllis

HIPPEASTRUM, ANNUAL

Consider that this exquisite yellow-green amaryllis produces two stems growing 2 feet high, each with four to six shooting starlike blooms. From large bulb to blossom takes about eight weeks. Plant in a container 2 inches or more wider than the bulb.

Why we love it: It's easy to grow outdoors in summer and performs well indoors in decorative containers during cold winter months.

9 Green Jewel coneflower

ECHINACEA PURPUREA, ZONES 3 TO 9

Coneflowers may not be rare, but green ones? They're hidden jewels. These easy-to-care-for perennials reach up to 24 inches and grow in large containers as well as garden beds. Their 4-inch blossoms make an appearance all summer and are beautiful cut flowers. While they tolerate partial shade, they also take the heat of full sun.

Why we love it: Fritillary, monarch, painted lady and swallowtail butterflies appreciate the nectar of coneflowers, and the seeds of spent flowers feed hungry birds such as blue jays, cardinals and goldfinches.

10 Green Spirit tulip

TULIPA, ZONES 3 TO 8

Creamy ivory petals with striations of lime green turn the heads of tulip lovers when this 2-foot beauty blooms in early spring. Plant bulbs in the fall in full sun or partial shade.

Why we love it: One word: stripes. Everyone knows vertical stripes are the most flattering.

GROW GREEN
More lime-hued flowers to love.

- Green Wizard rudbeckia
- Benary's Giant Lime zinnia
- Spring Green celosia
- Lady's mantle
- Coconut Lime coneflower
- Lime Sorbet columbine
- Lime Frost daylily

Let large hostas, like Mama Mia, be a focal point.

HOSTAS ADD MORE than just a welcome splash of color to shade gardens, they offer super low maintenance and major wildlife benefits. It can be challenging to incorporate the big, leafy, shade-loving perennial into a landscape. Help maximize your hosta's potential with these tips.

1. GROUP SIMILAR VARIETIES Try to cluster multiple specimens of the same cultivar for a put-together look. By massing them together, you give them more visual weight so they don't end up looking like an afterthought.

2. MAKE A FOCAL POINT A hosta that's big enough can be a solitary focal point and an exception to the clustering rule. Surround it with plenty of companions to create a stage for the plant. A solid-colored hosta makes a more natural-looking partner for other plants.

3. ALWAYS USE VARIEGATION WISELY Variegated hostas are tailor-made for lining a path. They not only look good, they serve a practical purpose: The bright, patterned leaves are easy to spot at night—making the route safer. Just be cautious when bunching unrelated variegated varieties together or it can look a bit chaotic. Pick one and repeat for emphasis.

4. REPEAT YOURSELF Planting a specific variety (or color) in a few areas helps tie the garden together. Similar plants lead the eye from foreground to midground to background in a pleasing way. If you're using multiple varieties, break them up in clusters of threes or fives so they carry more weight. The repeating effect will be more appealing.

Designing with Hostas

Bring out the best in these easy-to-grow favorites.

A group of different hostas creates a natural and full look.

5. KEEP IT NEAT Some gardeners prefer to remove the flower stalks to emphasize the foliage. If you choose to let them grow, snip them off when they're past their prime. Many hostas offer good fall color, but unsightly blooms detract from the picture. Plus, old leaves and plant residue harbor foliage-destroying slugs. One way to discourage the pests: Clean up debris every spring and replace with crushed eggshells or coarse sand.

6. MIX TEXTURES Texture is important in a garden of foliage plants because there's often less color to draw the eye. Pair strong broadleaf hostas with something wispy for interesting textural contrast. Ferns are a natural choice, as they enjoy the same growing conditions as hostas.

Try to find a fern that matches the color of the hosta.

7. GO AU NATURALE Hostas belong in a lush, shady oasis, not a barren garden. Create this effect by picking a big, bold hosta as the centerpiece and back it up with some other large broadleaf plants. Then surround with colorful flowering plants of various sizes and habits. Aim for abundant and full, not crowded. Create visual breaks with rocks, a log or garden art.

8. BRIGHTEN SHADOWS Lighten up the dark corners of your garden by incorporating some variegated hostas. These plants practically glow in the dark. Blue-green hostas are also a great choice, as their white flowers add even more light in summer.

DIVIDE AND CONQUER

For best results, divide hostas every three or four years, preferably in spring as foliage starts to emerge. Or divide in early fall if there is time for plants to reestablish themselves before winter.

HERE'S HOW:
Dig up a clump and separate it by hand, or use a sharp spade if clumps are large. Replant fist-sized sections or individual plantlets, leaving enough space for plants to mature.

Classic Beauties

Fun colors, small statures and long-lasting blooms—check out the hydrangea scene and six of the best species for your backyard.

1 Southern favorites, bigleaf hydrangeas are now available in reblooming varieties, giving gardeners in the North a chance to enjoy them.

2 The Tuff Stuff mountain hydrangea is a reblooming type. It flowers in spring on old wood and again on new wood.

HYDRANGEAS ARE HOT—and understandably so. It's not every day that gardeners find a shrub as colorful and easygoing as your average annual. Most hydrangeas bloom for months at a time and look lovely even as the flowers fade. They also make stunning cut flowers, fresh or dried.

Tuff Stuff mountain hydrangea

"People love hydrangeas because they're easy to grow and deliver loads of flowers all summer," says Natalie Carmolli, marketing and public relations specialist for Spring Meadow Nursery, growers of Proven Winners ColorChoice Shrubs. "They are also useful in a variety of settings as foundation plants or hedging, or planted on their own as a spectacular specimen plant."

In the U.S., six species of hydrangeas are popular, most of which have large to very large flower clusters, making them easy to appreciate from a distance. Those clusters come in a variety of shapes, including round mopheads, frilly lacecaps and showy cone shapes. Depending on the species and cultivar, flowers may be white, red, pink, blue or lime green, and the colors often change come autumn.

Among the six species, "smooth hydrangeas are incredibly easy to grow," Natalie says. "They are super cold hardy down to USDA Zone 3."

3 Little Quick Fire panicle hydrangea blooms a month earlier than others.

One of her favorites is the line of Incrediball hydrangeas. "If you are familiar with the classic white Annabelle hydrangea, you'll love Incrediball hydrangea," she says. "It has massive white blooms held up on sturdy stems, so they don't flop over as Annabelle tends to do."

Bigleaf hydrangeas are the plants most people gravitate to, especially cultivars with pink flowers (seen in soils with high pH) or blue flowers (soils with low pH). However, bigleaf hydrangeas wilt quickly if the soil dries out in summer, and they may not flower reliably in colder regions. Panicle hydrangeas are a better alternative for many gardeners.

"If you have lots of sun and need a drought-tolerant plant, you'll find

4 Use climbing hydrangeas to cover buildings, fences or arbors.

that panicle hydrangeas fare better than other types of hydrangeas," Natalie says. "They are also reliable bloomers that flower on new wood, making them a low-maintenance option for Zone 3 gardens." Natalie recommends Fire Light, which is packed with florets that transform from pure white to pink and then finish a pomegranate red.

Care and Maintenance

It's best to plant hydrangeas in moist, well-draining soil (they do not like wet feet). With shallow roots, they tend to dry out rather quickly, so a 2- to 3-inch layer of shredded bark mulch is helpful. All hydrangeas need some sunlight for best flowering, ideally in the morning, but oakleaf hydrangeas tolerate more shade than others.

Hydrangeas grow in a wide range of climates, but some are a little better suited to extreme temperatures than others. Panicle hydrangeas such as Limelight and the smaller Little Lime are the most adaptable to any climate, thriving in areas where others might struggle. The showy bigleaf hydrangeas and oakleaf hydrangeas typically don't do as well with temperature extremes, preferring the midrange zones. Smooth hydrangeas are cold hardy down to Zone 3 but do not like extreme heat.

What's New

COLOR: Smooth hydrangeas are now available in a variety of colors. Incrediball Blush is silvery pink; the Invincibelle series boasts pink, ruby and pink-mauve hues; and Lime Rickey shines with deep green flowers. These new, trendy cultivars have been bred with stronger stems to prevent flopping.

SAVE YOUR BOUNTY
Follow these steps to dry and preserve flowers.

- Wait until blooms start to fade and petals become less supple and more paperlike.
- Cut 12- to 18-inch stems and remove any leaves or foliage.
- Place in a vase of water, making sure flower heads aren't crowded.
- Keep the vase indoors, away from direct sunlight, for several weeks until stems are stiff.
- Use in bouquets, wreaths or other flower arrangements.

COMMON HYDRANGEAS

Six species to look for at the garden center:

1. Bigleaf (*Hydrangea macrophylla*)
2. Mountain (*H. serrata*)
3. Panicle (*H. paniculata*)
4. Climbing (*H. petiolaris*)
5. Oakleaf (*H. quercifolia*)
6. Smooth (*H. arborescens*)

SIZE: Hydrangeas are usually big and brassy, but plant breeders are working on compact varieties. If you're in the market for a bit of a smaller plant, look for Bobo panicle hydrangea, Tiny Tuff Stuff mountain hydrangea, Mini Penny bigleaf hydrangea and Invincibelle Wee White smooth hydrangea. "Wee White is a huge game changer because of its diminutive size," Natalie says. "Topping out at just 2½ feet, this is an ideal hydrangea for use in containers and in areas where the typical larger-sized hydrangea just isn't an option."

REBLOOMING: While hydrangeas are known for long-lasting blooms, work is being done to encourage reblooming among bigleaf and mountain varieties. The Tuff Stuff series starts blooming in early summer, producing new buds and blooms until frost. "Our newest variety is Tuff Stuff Ah-Ha mountain hydrangea," Natalie says. "It's a strong rebloomer, with huge waterlilylike double florets that are blue or pink depending on the soil."

5 Gatsby Pink oakleaf hydrangea is a native grown for fall color.

6 Invincibelle Wee White smooth hydrangea blooms for months.

Colorful Winter Plants

Add interest to frosty gardens with hardy, cold-blooming perennials.

1

EARLY BLOOMER
Hellebores first blossom around the holidays in warm regions, depending on the species. Expect plants to bloom in early spring in colder climates.

1 Hellebore

HELLEBORUS, ZONES 4 TO 9

Cold-weather gardens welcome hellebore's cup-shaped blossoms. With numerous colors, and heights ranging from 1 to 2 feet, this lovely and distinctive bloomer is sure to enhance most any landscape. Hellebore is a perennial that loves moisture and shade, and you'll probably wish it bloomed all year-round.

Why we love it: It's easy to grow and one of the first flowers to emerge in late winter or early spring.

2 Rugosa rose

ROSA RUGOSA, ZONES 2 TO 7

Large, low-maintenance shrubs grow to 6 feet high and wide. The plant's secret winter weapon is its large, tomato-shaped red hips, which show up after it blooms. Wait to prune until early spring and avoid planting in wet soil. It is considered invasive in some areas, so research before planting.

Why we love it: It has dazzling flowers in early summer, fabulous color in autumn and bright hips in winter.

3 Winter heath

ERICA CARNEA, ZONES 5 TO 7

This evergreen low-growing plant will treat you to an abundance of little purple-pink flowers throughout most of winter and into early spring. Winter heath grows in 6- to 9-inch mounds and creates a dense ground cover over time. It prefers acidic, perfectly drained soil, but it's more tolerant than other heaths.

Why we love it: Glimpsing its small, urn-shaped flowers poking through the snow is delightful.

4 Snowdrop

GALANTHUS, ZONES 3 TO 8

Popping up in late winter, snowdrop's bright green leaves send the message loud and clear that spring is right around the corner. For a large collection of these 4- to 6-inch plants, simply lift and divide bulbs after they bloom but before the foliage dies back.

Why we love it: Snowdrops are nice because they are low-maintenance and especially attractive scattered throughout natural gardens and under deciduous trees and shrubs.

5 Dwarf iris

VARIETIES INCLUDE *IRIS DANFORDIAE* AND
I. RETICULATA, ZONES 3 TO 9

Reaching just 3 to 9 inches in height, this
group of diminutive irises brings bursts of
jewel-toned color to late winter and early spring
landscapes. Native to Turkey and Iran, they
prefer well-draining soil and do best in full sun
or partial shade. For an even earlier show, force
the bulbs indoors in October or November.
Why we love it: The blooms offer beautiful
early color accompanied by a wonderful fragrance.

6 Early scilla

SCILLA MISCHTSCHENKOANA, ZONES 4 TO 7

If you're into cool hues, seek out early scilla. This compact
green plant sports star-shaped white blossoms striped with
blue. They grow in full sun to light shade and spread by
offsets and self-seeding. Plant early scilla bulbs in autumn
for a spectacular sight come late winter to early spring.
Why we love it: It's a snap to maintain and often continues
to flower annually.

7 Ornamental cabbage

BRASSICA OLERACEA, ANNUAL

This unusual ornamental flaunts vibrant shades of purple,
green, blue, red, pink or white well into winter. Grow in full
sun to partial shade. In Zone 7 and warmer, the cabbage is
a biennial plant. Try its colorful cousin, ornamental kale,
for similar results.
Why we love it: The lower that temps plunge, the more
vivid this vegetable's unique colors become.

8 Scotch heather

CALLUNA VULGARIS, ZONES 5 TO 7

Celebrated throughout Europe, heather is often forgotten in North America. This versatile flower boasts color in every season; just grow in acidic soil. Where snowfall is light, insulate heather with mulch and pine branches.

Why we love it: This beauty lends appeal with florets in summer and autumn, and gorgeous foliage in winter.

9 Crocus

VARIETIES INCLUDE *CROCUS ANCYRENSIS* AND *C. TOMMASINIANUS*, ZONES 3 TO 8

In late winter, keep your eyes peeled for these purple, yellow and white flowers poking out of a bed of mulch or beneath a snowy blanket. Plant large drifts of corms in fall for stunning color the next season.

Why we love it: Crocuses are known for their strong scent, and help support and attract the first bees and other pollinators emerging from hibernation.

10 Prairie dropseed

SPOROBOLUS HETEROLEPIS, ZONES 3 TO 9

This grass's fine-textured, hairlike leaves cluster in green mounds 2 to 3 feet tall and wide. When its seeds mature in autumn, they drop to the ground from their hulls, giving the plant its common name. The grass provides beautiful structure in winter and grows in a range of soils. For best results, plant in sandy or loamy plots in full sun. It is drought-tolerant and native to many areas in the U.S.

Why we love it: Thin strands fade to light bronze in the winter, creating a wonderful border or foundation plant.

Blooms Galore

Flowers are the true stars of the growing season, and they shine in these reader snapshots.

My wife knows sunflowers are my favorite, so she planted a patch in our yard for me to photograph. I waited for the perfect day to get started—one with a blue sky and no wind. I love the echo of the bloom in the background in this shot.

Dale Aspy
MARIETTA, GEORGIA

With my trusty Nikon D5100 in hand, I headed out to photograph flowers early one morning while the dew still dotted the petals. I thought this purple iris bloom was just absolutely breathtaking.

Lynn Erdely
GREENSBORO,
NORTH CAROLINA

A short stop one afternoon at Thomas Jefferson's Monticello estate resulted in this lucky shot of cherry blossoms. The vivid color of the blue sky provided the perfect background for the delicate petals. I happily continued on my way to the National Cherry Blossom Festival.

Shannon Anderson
ELIZABETHTOWN, KENTUCKY

I visited a dahlia farm in Oregon last summer. This was one of their experimental varieties, and I absolutely fell in love with this small flower. It's simple and elegant, with a great color combo. I just felt like it had personality.

Lori Naanes
GOSPORT, INDIANA

This photo of a purple water lily represents summer for me. The vibrant colors of these beautiful blooms catch your eye as they stand out among the floating pads.

Marlana McTague
BROOKSVILLE, FLORIDA

While practicing with my Canon 70D in macro mode on coneflowers, a bee flew in for a landing, which gave me an impromptu two-subject photo shoot! I was super happy with how it turned out, thanks to my photo bomber.

Anna Morrison
LOWELL, MASSACHUSETTS

This is one of my best flower photos to date! While photographing butterflies one day, I randomly snapped a quick shot of this daylily bloom. When I saw how well it turned out, I was so delighted!

Anne Jensen
TABER, ALBERTA

Despite harsh afternoon conditions and lighting, I captured this unique view of a clematis bloom during my visit to the South Carolina Botanical Garden in Clemson, South Carolina.

Mike Dinkens
CANTON, GEORGIA

Last summer a very beautiful passionflower vine rewarded me with daily blooms. This photo shows the unique details of this stunning flower. It's so special to me because it gives a mystical quality to my landscape.

Ronald Greene
CHESTERLAND, OHIO

Several years ago my mom gave me a clematis vine. I planted it next to the lattice under my deck. It never had more than a half dozen flowers in any year, and I was ready to remove it. Mom encouraged me to be patient and give it another season. She was right! My patience paid off the following year when the plant produced nearly 100 blossoms. I'm so happy I followed her advice.

Mike Droppleman
NORTON, OHIO

Butterfly Life

Get to know these backyard stunners and the flowers they crave, and discover the fascinating world of caterpillars.

CHAPTER 6

Delicately in Focus

Readers captured the brief moments when these fast-flying garden guests paused among summer foliage.

This American lady visited my garden a few summers ago. I love this close-up shot because it shows the intricate details of the butterfly's wings and eye. The purple coneflower also provides an interesting contrast to the blue-green background.

Katerina Kretsch BRISTOL, CONNECTICUT

I took this photo of a skipper the summer I got my first digital Canon DSLR. I never knew what these tiny butterflies looked like up close! It was neat to catch all the details, such as the way the light shines on its eye and proboscis and through its wings.

Gina Howell
HUNTINGTON, WEST VIRGINIA

Sunflowers always seem to please everyone, from squirrels to grackles, goldfinches and chickadees. On this particular day, three monarchs went from bloom to bloom, enjoying the flowers. It reminded me that I don't have to leave my yard to experience the beauty of nature.

Mary-Ann Ingrao
ANGOLA, NEW YORK

"Magnificent" and "royal" are spot-on descriptions for the regal fritillary. I took the photo as this one sipped nectar from a butterfly weed in my backyard. This visitor is becoming scarce because of a decrease in habitat, making the sighting even more special.

Gail Huddle
McPHERSON, KANSAS

An eastern tiger swallowtail eluded me the first time one visited my garden, and I lost my chance at a nice photo. But another one was gracious enough to come and stay awhile. I took many shots and captured this special moment with a sunflower.

Elisabeth Stuart COLUMBIA, SOUTH CAROLINA

It's challenging to photograph butterflies that are constantly on the move, so when this cabbage white finally landed on my butterfly bush, I took advantage of the opportunity. It may not have the colors and patterns of some fellow fliers, but I think it has a beauty all its own.

Barbara Houlihan MADISON, WISCONSIN

I captured this photo of a white peacock butterfly with my Canon EOS at the Brookfield Zoo near Chicago. It was my first time checking out the butterfly exhibit there, and all the different kinds were amazing!

Heidi Kelly
PLAINFIELD, ILLINOIS

Giant
swallowtail

The Bold & Beautiful

Zebra
swallowtail

Big, vibrant and abundant, swallowtail butterflies bring
a flurry of eye-catching activity to any backyard.

Anise
swallowtails

SWOOPING OVER MEADOWS and pausing on blooms, swallowtails draw attention with their large size and striking colors. They get their name from the extended tails on their hindwings. This feature makes them more buoyant in flight but, interestingly, not all swallowtails possess it.

With more than 500 species fluttering over six continents, swallowtails are a diverse family. Most are tropical, but about 25 kinds are found regularly in the United States and Canada. No matter where you live, you can see them during the warmer months of the year.

Aptly Named

Many swallowtails have colorful names that help with identification. For example, the tiger group is bright yellow with narrow black stripes. Three species in this group—eastern, western and Canadian—are separated by range, but among the three of them, they're found everywhere from Florida and Southern California to northern Canada and Alaska. A similar flier with a bit of a fancier shape, the two-tailed swallowtail, is a very common sight in the West.

Many butterfly lovers consider the zebra swallowtail, so prevalent in Eastern forests, the most beautiful. It's striped black and white, as the name suggests, and has red accents. Very long tails on the hindwings give it an especially graceful, flowing flight.

However, the giant swallowtail butterfly is not the largest member of the family, as its name implies—some eastern tigers are actually larger—though the giant is still big enough to be impressive. Giant swallowtails live mainly in Southern states, but a few wander far north every summer, reaching southern Canada.

Pipevine swallowtail

Black swallowtail caterpillar

Pipevine swallowtail caterpillar

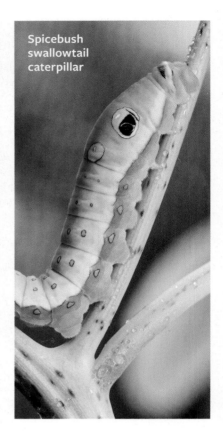

Spicebush swallowtail caterpillar

Neat Caterpillars

Swallowtails are large butterflies, so naturally their caterpillars, or larvae, grow to be pretty good-sized. Many have beautiful or strange color patterns.

The giant swallowtail caterpillar has a smeary black and white pattern, and when it's still small, it's easy to miss because it looks like bird droppings. The pipevine caterpillar is dark reddish to black and covered with orange spikes. In some species, such as the tiger and spicebush swallowtails, the caterpillar is green with two large round spots on the swollen front end that look like the eyes of a snake. This may startle birds enough to leave the larvae alone.

Swallowtail larvae have one more trick. They all have a Y-shaped organ called an osmeterium tucked into a cavity just behind their heads. If the caterpillar is threatened, the fleshy orange osmeterium pops out. It looks a little like the forked tongue of a snake, and it carries a smell that's foul enough to repel some predators.

Models and Mimics

Monarch butterflies are famous for having caterpillars that eat milkweed. This habit allows them to take in chemicals that make even the adults taste bad to predators. The pipevine swallowtail, common in Southern states, uses the same chemical protection. Its larvae feed on pipevine plants, and bitter compounds from those plants stay in the adults. When a bird grabs a pipevine swallowtail, it gets a mouthful of unpleasant taste and learns to look for other caterpillars for food.

Predators pass up several other butterfly species simply because they look similar to pipevines. This includes the spicebush and others—as well as some completely unrelated butterflies, like the red-spotted purple.

Some female eastern tiger swallowtails may use this defense. They can either be yellow, like the males of their species, or dark to mimic the bitter pipevine swallowtail. The dark form is found mainly in the South, where such mimicry is more likely to be effective because birds there have experienced the toxic taste of the pipevine.

The Right Plants

Swallowtails are attracted to a wide variety of blooms for nectar. They may visit any garden, but to keep them coming around, the most important thing is to provide host plants for their caterpillars.

Many larvae live on and eat leaves of only certain trees and shrubs. Zebra swallowtail caterpillars mainly feed on pawpaw trees. Spicebush swallowtails favor the spicebush and sassafras. Eastern tiger swallowtails go for several kinds of trees, including ash, wild cherry and tulip tree. Canadian tiger swallowtails can't eat tulip tree leaves, instead favoring aspen and birch. Giant swallowtail larvae feed on various plants in the citrus family.

With so many choosy appetites, it's a good idea to research which swallowtails live in your area before deciding on what garden plants to try.

The easiest members of the family to attract are black swallowtails in the East and Southwest, and anise swallowtails in the West. The beautifully colored, striped and spotted caterpillars of these common butterflies feed on many plants in the parsley family, so plant more to share. Then enjoy watching the swallowtail caterpillars grow, knowing you're supporting local butterfly populations.

Parnassian swallowtail

MOUNTAIN MARVELS

Another branch of the family is usually found in high altitudes.

A unique subset of the swallowtail family, the parnassians are tailless white butterflies with black marks and red spots. Most kinds live in the mountains of Asia and Europe, but five species are found in western North America, mostly in high mountains or on northern tundra. In the cool climates of the mountains, parnassians usually fly slowly and stay close to the ground.

Spicebush swallowtail

Fluttering Fritillaries

Look for glints of silver on large orange wings to spot these popular fliers.

I love to spend time in the fields and forest near my home, watching for winged insects and other wildlife. I planted purple coneflowers in my meadow, and the butterflies love them, especially the fritillaries.

Denise Tomasura
SWEET VALLEY, PENNSYLVANIA

One of my flower gardens is designed to attract hummingbirds and butterflies. Last year, the great spangled fritillaries were exceptionally numerous and visited the purple coneflowers the most.

Elisa Shaw
RED HOOK, NEW YORK

I am always on the lookout for beautiful flowers to photograph. One summer day I found thistle growing among the bushes and trees near our pond. As I was snapping away, a great spangled fritillary stopped to collect some nectar.

Cassandra Kaanana BRIXEY, MISSOURI

GREAT SPANGLED FRITILLARY

WINGSPAN
2⅛ to 3 inches.

DISTINCTIVE MARKINGS
Orange with black patterned marks. Yellow band and silver spots on underside of hindwings.

HABITAT
Open, moist-soiled meadows, woodlands, valleys and pastures.

CATERPILLAR
Black with orange-striped spines. Dormant in winter, feeds on violets in spring.

HOST PLANT
Violets.

BACKYARD FAVORITES
Adults sip nectar from Joe Pye weed, common milkweed, verbena and red clover. Females lay their eggs near violets, the only plants caterpillars eat.

DID YOU KNOW?
Great spangled caterpillars hatch in the fall, overwinter in that stage and then finally take their first bites of food in spring.

Grow a Butterfly Buffet

Pick the right nectar-filled plants and your garden will overflow with winged visitors.

Butterfly bush is a popular shrub for butterflies like this comma. But be careful. It's invasive in some areas of the country, so read up before planting or grow a noninvasive variety.

IMAGINE YOUR GARDEN filled with butterflies hovering over blooms of every hue, plus hummingbirds zipping by in a flash and busy bees whirring through the air with a quiet buzz. The birds and the bees are just another bonus in a butterfly-friendly world.

"Butterflies have a universal appeal," says Kathleen LaLiberte, a writer for New Jersey bulb grower Longfield Gardens. "Seeing these delicate, fanciful creatures dancing through the air in search of flowers can't help but lift your spirits." The good news is that with a little knowledge and effort, you can create a butterfly garden paradise!

"If you want your garden to be attractive to butterflies, think about two main things," Kathleen says. "First is flower choice. Some are naturally more appealing than others." Butterflies need plants that produce nectar for them to eat, but those plants come in a wide variety. Strive for a mix of heights, colors and exposures, as some butterflies actually prefer shade to sun.

KIDS LOVE BUTTERFLIES!

Butterfly gardening is a family-friendly activity, too. Start a journal together to log your sightings and draw pictures of your garden visitors. Go on a caterpillar hunt; follow the life cycle from start to finish. At the end of the summer, have kids help gather seeds and plan next season's adventure.

The second factor to consider is bloom time, says Kathleen. "Where I live, we start seeing butterflies at the end of May and the last ones leave in mid-October. Assemble a collection of plants that flower at different times during the growing season so your buffet is always open."

Round out the landscape with shelter, such as ornamental grasses or plants with thick foliage. Add some host plants caterpillars use, like milkweed and parsley. Avoid pesticides whenever possible, as they harm caterpillars and butterflies along with pests.

Finally, Kathleen says, "Our role as flower gardeners is about more than making the world beautiful. It's also about doing whatever we can to reduce our negative impact on the earth and help preserve biodiversity." A healthy butterfly garden is one of the greatest gifts you can give the earth...and yourself.

NECTAR FAVORITES

These nine easy-to-grow options will have your garden abuzz with butterflies.

1. SPEEDWELL

VERONICA SPICATA, ZONES 3 TO 8
The butterfly season kicks off in late spring when speedwell emerges. Dense spikes are covered in tiny nectar-rich flowers that may rebloom in summer.
Try: Ulster Blue Dwarf

2. ALLIUM

ALLIUM SPP., ZONES 4 TO 9
Would you believe these glorious globes are closely related to onions? It's true! Their unique appearance adds pizazz to the garden, and brings in butterflies by the dozen. **Try:** Gladiator

3. HOSTA

HOSTA SPP., ZONES 3 TO 9
Beloved for its broad-leaved foliage, hosta also attracts butterflies when it throws up bloom stalks covered in lavender or white flowers in mid- to late summer. **Try:** Lakeside Dragonfly

4. GLADIOLUS

GLADIOLUS SPP., ZONES 8 TO 11
The tropical blaze of gladiolus really ups the wow factor in any garden. In colder zones, lift the corms in fall to store for winter, or treat it as an annual and replant each spring. **Try:** Lumiere

5. CLEMATIS

CLEMATIS SPP., ZONES 3 TO 10
Every good butterfly garden needs a vine to grow along a fence or up a trellis, and clematis is both beautiful and easy to care for. Plant several varieties to ensure flowers all season long. **Try:** Miss Bateman/Red Cardinal plant combo

6. LIATRIS

LIATRIS SPP., ZONES 3 TO 10
Blazing star, or liatris, is a native wildflower that butterflies know and love. Fuzzy flowers appear in early fall, extending the butterfly garden season right up until frost. **Try:** Kobold

7. CROCOSMIA

CROCOSMIA SPP., ZONES 5 TO 9
Also known as sword lily, crocosmia sports bright red spikes that grow nearly 3 feet tall, drawing butterflies and hummingbirds throughout the season. **Try:** Lucifer

8. HELENIUM

HELENIUM SPP., ZONES 3 TO 9
A native wildflower that's perfect later in the season, helenium thrives on regular watering in well-draining soil. You'll be rewarded with blooms that are butterfly magnets from late summer to fall. **Try:** Moerheim Beauty

9. CHOCOLATE COSMOS

COSMOS ATROSANGUINEUS, ZONES 7 TO 11
A blossom that smells like chocolate and attracts butterflies might seem too good to be true, but chocolate cosmos are real—and spectacular. They love dry soil and lots of sun.

Open Invitation

Colorful, easy-to-grow plants for a butterfly-enticing garden.

1

SWEET TREAT
A great spangled fritillary gets its nectar fix from a butterfly weed flower cluster.

1 Butterfly weed

ASCLEPIAS TUBEROSA, ZONES 3 TO 9

Distinctive clusters of bright orange flowers are a must-stop destination for butterflies, especially monarchs and black swallowtails. After all, it didn't get its name for nothing. Butterfly weed grows 1 to 2½ feet tall and blooms from mid- to late summer. It tolerates dry soil and prefers plenty of sunshine.

Why we love it: The showy bright orange blooms are deer resistant and drought tolerant, and butterfly weed is easy to grow from seed and a super resilient pick—a major win!

2 Cleome

CLEOME HASSLERIANA, ANNUAL

This old-time garden favorite, also called spider flower, gets its common name from the long and threadlike flower stamens and elongated seedpods. Cultivars have white, pink, rose or purple flowers and quickly reach 5 to 6 feet tall. Newer cultivars, between 12 and 18 inches tall, are suitable for growing in containers.

Why we love it: Cleome is a bright, resilient flower that readily self-seeds new generations. In addition to butterflies, bees and hummingbirds also love it.

3 Pentas

PENTAS LANCEOLATA, ANNUAL

If you like butterflies, you simply must grow pentas. These bright annuals, also known as starflowers, are easy to spot from afar. Just look for the large clusters of starlike flowers in bright pinks, reds and whites. They're full of nectar and true butterfly magnets. And aside from being frost sensitive, they're pretty hardy. Shorter cultivars work well in pots, while taller pentas can be interspersed with other companions in beds.

Why we love it: The annual has the size and presence of a perennial.

4 Meadow blazing star

LIATRIS LIGULISTYLIS, ZONES 3 TO 8

While any liatris attracts pollinators, spindly meadow blazing star is one of the monarch butterfly's absolute favorite nectar sources. The long-lasting flowers range from rose to purple and appear in late summer on stalks reaching 4 to 6 feet high.

Why we love it: Very showy flowers pop up late in the growing season when color is needed; tall plants make butterfly viewing easy.

5 Phlox

PHLOX SPP., ZONES 3 TO 9

Grow several forms of phlox for big impact, from the spring-blooming ground cover moss phlox (*P. subulata*) to the lanky summer stalwart garden phlox (*P. paniculata*). Growing different phlox species extends the butterfly season—and gives you more flower colors, including white, purple, lavender, pink and bicolors.

Why we love it: Many phlox are nicely fragrant, and some are even resistant to powdery mildew.

Sky Blue Marvel salvia

6 Salvia

SALVIA SPP., ZONES 3 TO 10 OR ANNUAL

Whether you're growing the popular bedding annuals or a taller perennial type, salvia never fails to impress—or to attract butterflies, hummingbirds and bees. Fortunately, it's got true staying power, and even some perennial types have long-lasting flowers. Salvias are very forgiving and easy to grow, tolerating drought and clay soil.

Why we love it: Brightly hued flower spikes stand out among companion plants.

7 Swamp milkweed

ASCLEPIAS INCARNATA, ZONES 3 TO 9

Like other milkweeds, it doesn't look like much—until it blooms. Then you're treated to bright purplish pink flower heads rising 5 feet in the air. You can't miss them and, fortunately, neither can the butterflies. The foliage is also a critical food source for monarch caterpillars.

Why we love it: It features a long bloom time and impressive size, and grows well in wet sites.

8 Coreopsis

COREOPSIS SPP., ZONES 3 TO 9

Some cultivars have rose, white or bicolor flowers, but coreopsis is known to go for the gold—offering a preponderance of golden yellow flowers in summer. Keep it deadheaded for continuous color. Some species bloom in early summer, others in late summer. Plant both types to keep the butterflies coming all season long.

Why we love it: Find it in various heights to fit everything from diminutive rock gardens to tall prairie plantings.

9 New Jersey tea

CEANOTHUS AMERICANUS, ZONES 3 TO 8

This tough little shrub sneers at dry, rocky soils and drought, thanks to thick roots that penetrate deeply into the soil. The dried leaves were a tea substitute in Colonial times, but the plant has a different purpose today. It covers rocky sites and offers butterfly-attracting flowers in late spring.

Why we love it: Compact and easy to grow, it is resistant to pest and disease problems.

10 Aster

ASTER OR *SYMPHYOTRICHUM* SPP., ZONES 3 TO 10

These hardy perennials make a great companion to mums and offer late-season sustenance to butterflies, particularly fall-migrating monarchs. The nectar-rich, daisylike flowers come in a range of vibrant colors, including white, purple, blue and pink. Sizes vary from 1 to 4 feet, depending on species and cultivar.

Why we love it: Aster is simple to grow, drought tolerant and full of color in late summer and early fall, when other perennials are spent.

Milkweed Lovers

Attract more monarchs with the plants they can't resist!

I have created a gorgeous butterfly garden over the years to invite as many species as possible. They all seem to gravitate to the coneflowers, even though I grow many of their favorites. Monarchs are rare guests in my garden, so it was extra special when this one visited me.

Maryann Massar JOHNSON CITY, NEW YORK

I fell in love
with monarchs when
I found a chrysalis and
watched this butterfly
slowly emerge and fly
away. It made me think
about the importance
of learning to soar
through changes.
I lost my husband
a few years ago and
have embraced this
meaningful lesson.

Carol Manglos-Foster
ONEMO, VIRGINIA

DID YOU KNOW?
Monarchs fly up to 2,000
miles to their wintering
grounds, clipping away
at just 12 mph.

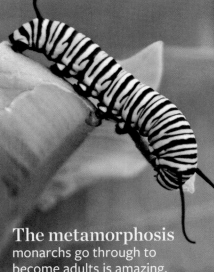

The metamorphosis
monarchs go through to
become adults is amazing.
They rely on milkweed for
survival, and with habitat
disappearing, it's more
important than ever for
gardeners to plant it.

Jenny Miner IRMA, WISCONSIN

MONARCH

WINGSPAN
3½ to 4¾ inches.

DISTINCTIVE MARKINGS
Bright orange with multiple black
veins. Wings are edged in black
with white speckles.

HABITAT
Cities to rural fields and mountain
pastures. When breeding, they
prefer open areas.

CATERPILLAR
White with yellow and black stripes.
Two sets of long black filaments.

HOST PLANT
Caterpillars eat milkweed exclusively.

NECTAR FAVORITES
Showy, common or swamp
milkweed, heliotrope and
butterfly weed.

QUIRKY QUALITY
Bright orange wings let predators
know they are poisonous.

Crazy Cool
Caterpillars

This caterpillar turns into that regal moth!

Get the lowdown on these bizarre crawly creatures—from plump and stripy to horned and dangerous. And see the adult moths and butterflies they transform into.

REGAL MOTH

Nicknamed hickory horned devils, these caterpillars grow up to 6 inches long. Despite their fearsome look and size, they're harmless to humans. But for potential predators, bright colors and gigantic horns are a clear sign to stay away. When disturbed, these bugs make a loud rapid clicking noise for good measure.

RANGE:
Eastern United States

HOST PLANTS:
Hickory, sycamore, walnut and persimmon

REGAL
◄ CATERPILLAR
   MOTH ►

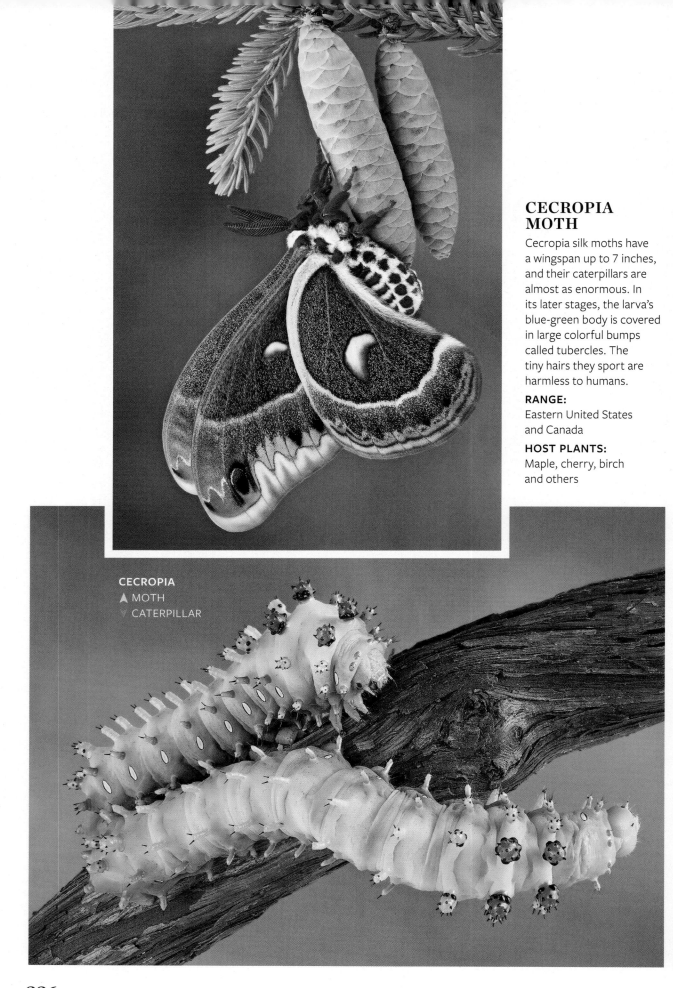

CECROPIA MOTH

Cecropia silk moths have a wingspan up to 7 inches, and their caterpillars are almost as enormous. In its later stages, the larva's blue-green body is covered in large colorful bumps called tubercles. The tiny hairs they sport are harmless to humans.

RANGE:
Eastern United States and Canada

HOST PLANTS:
Maple, cherry, birch and others

CECROPIA
▲ MOTH
▼ CATERPILLAR

SPICEBUSH SWALLOWTAIL

▲ CATERPILLAR
➤ BUTTERFLY

SPICEBUSH SWALLOWTAIL

What appear to be giant eyes are really just eyespots to fool predators into thinking this insect is much larger than it is. These creatures roll leaves around their bodies to create safe shelters to eat and rest. Later stages of this caterpillar are bright green, turning a brilliant orange just before the final molt into a chrysalis.

RANGE:
Eastern United States

HOST PLANTS:
Spicebush, camphor, sassafras, sweetbay and tulip tree

ISABELLA TIGER
➤ CATERPILLAR
MOTH

ISABELLA TIGER MOTH

Woolly bear is the popular name for Isabella tiger moth caterpillars. Folklore says the wider the dark stripes, the harder the coming winter. In reality, the dark brown band on woolly bears merely widens as they grow throughout the season. Isabella tiger moths overwinter as caterpillars, freezing solid and thawing in the spring to continue eating and growing.

RANGE:
United States and lower Canada

HOST PLANTS:
Generalist feeder—eats a large variety of plants and trees

IO MOTH

In nature, bright colors often signal to predators that an animal is toxic, and that's definitely the case with io (pronounced EYE-oh) caterpillars. The bright green spikes are covered in tiny hairs that release toxins when touched. It causes excruciating pain in humans and other predators, so hands off!

RANGE:
Eastern United States

HOST PLANTS:
Hackberry, willow, redbud, mesquite and more

IO
▼ CATERPILLAR
➤ MOTH

POLYPHEMUS MOTH

This unique caterpillar boasts a lime green hue and geometric shape instead of a rounded body. The adult moth is one of the largest in North America, with a wingspan of nearly 6 inches. Silk moths like the polyphemus don't eat when they are adults, so their larvae are especially voracious. Polyphemus caterpillars grow up to 4 inches long.

RANGE:
United States and lower Canada

HOST PLANTS:
Birch, willow, maple, oak and others

ATALA
HAIRSTREAK
▲ CATERPILLAR
▼ BUTTERFLY

ATALA HAIRSTREAK

As you might guess, its bright colors are a clear warning—this little creature carries toxins in its body, but it's safe to touch. Atala butterflies were nearly wiped out in the 20th century by habitat destruction, but they are making a comeback in southern Florida and spreading north. Newly hatched caterpillars are light tan and relatively unimpressive, but they grow into their fantastic color in a day or two.

RANGE:
Southern Florida and a few Caribbean islands

HOST PLANTS:
Coontie and other cycad plants

QUESTION MARK

This insect is carpeted in tiny, nonvenomous spikes that make it an unfortunate mouthful for most predators to swallow. They also are smaller than most larvae shown here, topping out at about 1¾ inches long, and varying in color. The caterpillars are black with white or yellow lines and sport barbs ranging from yellow to orange to black. You're most likely to find these spiny bugs in yards next to moist woodlands.

RANGE:
Eastern and southern United States, west to Arizona

HOST PLANTS:
Elm, hackberry, nettles and hops

QUESTION MARK
▲ MOTH
▼ CATERPILLAR

CHAPTER 7

Ask the Experts

Our pros, Kenn and Kimberly Kaufman and Melinda Myers, help you solve common backyard dilemmas.

Q Usually robin nests in my yard have three eggs, but last year I saw eight. Is that normal or are multiple robins using the same nest?

Sommer Raines CONNERSVILLE, INDIANA

Kenn and Kimberly: When robins find a good site for a nest, they sometimes come back and use it repeatedly, as you've seen. But they typically lay three or four eggs, seldom a clutch of five. When a nest holds six to eight robin eggs, two females probably are laying eggs in the nest—perhaps competing for the site until one gives up. So what you've found is truly unusual, and it's an example of the fascinating discoveries that come with careful observation.

Q I planted Queen of the Night tulips and Poet's daffodils about 10 years ago. Now they only produce foliage and no blooms. Why is this happening?

Sue Gronholz BEAVER DAM, WISCONSIN

Melinda: Many new tulip hybrids, like the Queen of the Night shown here, put on a glorious show the first few years and then stop blooming. Consider them short-lived flowers that give you an opportunity to try something new every few years. Or switch to species tulips that tend to grow, spread and flower for many years. Try digging, dividing and replanting Poet's daffodils. Do this in spring after they have had several months to grow, or mark the location and divide them in the fall when you plant other bulbs. Make sure the daffodils receive at least partial sun for ideal flowering. This is often enough to stimulate blooms. Perhaps also try this technique to stimulate tulips—if it fails, you've only lost some time.

Q When I purchase live mealworms they come in a container full of shavings. Should I put the shavings into the feeder?

Joan Tornai PALO CEDRO, CALIFORNIA

Kenn and Kimberly: So many birds love to eat live mealworms, but storing and offering them presents some challenges. It's difficult to separate the worms from the shavings completely, so you often end up with this material in the feeder—whether you want to or not. It isn't necessary to add the shavings to the feeder, but it won't hurt either.

Q I'm new to attracting purple martins. Can you give me some guidance on choosing and setting up a birdhouse?

Cindy Phelps LOUISBURG, NORTH CAROLINA

Kenn and Kimberly: The abundance of choices for purple martins can be daunting. To get started, we recommend a house made of aluminum (painted white) or very thick white plastic, with at least 12 compartments. Wooden houses work, but they're heavy, which is a drawback as the house should be mounted 12 to 18 feet above the ground. You need to be able to open each compartment individually for cleaning. For mounting, it's best to have a sturdy pole with a pulley system so the house can be easily raised and lowered. The Purple Martin Conservation Association (*purplemartin.org*) offers a wealth of information on attracting these birds.

Q Is it better to transplant perennials in the fall or spring?

Judy Roberts GRAYTOWN, OHIO

Melinda: For the best results, transplant spring-flowering perennials in late summer or early fall. Move fall-blooming perennials in spring, and summer-blooming ones in spring or fall. The more you garden, the more you'll realize it's possible to move perennials whenever it's needed, as long as you provide proper post-transplant care.

DINNER WITH FRIENDS
It's common to see northern cardinals eating with their mates, but they're not opposed to sharing a meal with other bird species.

Q It seems more birds than usual come to my feeder when it's raining. Why?

Jody Kreider MURRIETA, CALIFORNIA

Kenn and Kimberly: Wild birds pay close attention to the weather at all times and with good reason, because it has such a huge impact on their survival. We often notice that birds feed more actively when storms are approaching. They may swarm the feeders, almost frantic to eat as much as possible, when a big blizzard is coming in, but even a gentle rain seems to boost their appetites. Apparently they have an instinct to fill up when there's the threat of any kind of weather condition that may make food harder to find.

Q What kind of milkweed should I grow, and where do I buy it?

Leo Patt OSHKOSH, WISCONSIN

Melinda: The monarch caterpillar's preferred food is common milkweed, but it feeds on other members of the milkweed family, too. Common milkweed is a bit aggressive, so be prepared to give it room or weed out unwanted plants. It spreads by seed and underground rhizomes. Remove pods before the seeds are released if you want to limit seedlings in next year's garden. Sullivant's (*Asclepias sullivantii*, below) looks similar to common milkweed but is a bit less aggressive. Look for the best milkweed options at native plant nurseries, perennial plant nurseries and some independent garden centers.

Q I spotted this butterfly or moth on a pink lady's slipper orchid. What is it?

Cindy Archer MOORESVILLE, NORTH CAROLINA

Kenn and Kimberly: Angular wings, held out to the sides at rest, are typical of the geometer moths. Geometer moths make up a very large and diverse family, with more than 1,400 species in North America. Some of them are very hard to identify, but the one in your photo looks like a good match for the white slant-line (*Tetracis cachexiata*), a geometer that's widespread east of the Rockies.

Q This creature landed on my window screen. A few days later, an exoskeleton remained as if it had molted. What is it?

Robert LaPointe PHILLIPS, WISCONSIN

Kenn and Kimberly: That's a fine photo of an adult mayfly. In their larval form, these fascinating insects live underwater in lakes and streams for one or two years, sometimes longer. After they crawl up out of the water to emerge as winged adults, they live for only a day or two. Adults don't have functioning mouthparts so they can't eat; they live just long enough to mate and for the females to lay eggs in the water. And you're right, they do molt. Other winged insects, like dragonflies or butterflies, only molt their exoskeletons (or "skins") while they're still growing in the larval or caterpillar stage. Mayflies are unique in molting once after they reach their winged adult form, which is all the more surprising since their adult lives are so brief.

Q What's the best way to care for pre-planted hanging flower baskets all season? Should I pick off dead, wilted flowers? Sun or no sun?

Shawn Berto IRONWOOD, MICHIGAN

Melinda: Professional growers do an excellent job of creating beautiful baskets packed full of flowering plants. They keep them looking their best with regular deadheading, strategically timed pruning and season-long fertilization. You can do the same. Remove faded flowers on annuals that perform best when deadheaded. Prune leggy stems back to above a healthy set of leaves to keep the plants compact. Stagger pruning, allowing some of the plants to continue flowering while others are clipped back. Use a slow-release fertilizer to provide weeks of nutrients, or apply a quick-release fertilizer every week or two. Read and follow label directions for sun exposure and fertilizer.

Princess Alexandra of Kent shrub rose from David Austin Roses

Q Ants swarmed the buds on my rosebush. Is this normal? Why are they doing this?

Ann Hillebrand KENT, WASHINGTON

Melinda: The ants are after the sweet nectar inside the rosebud. They aren't causing damage to the plant so there is no need to treat. Just be sure to check the blooms for ants before you bring them indoors. It's common to find ants on the buds of fragrant peonies as well. Contrary to an old garden myth, ants are not needed to open the peony flowers; they are just interested in the nectar.

Ants are also found on plants where aphids are feeding. The aphids suck plant juices and secrete the excess as a clear sticky substance called honeydew. Gardeners often see the ants first and then discover the aphids feeding on their plants. Insecticidal soap is an organic option for controlling the aphids and will help wash off the honeydew.

Q This plant grew in a pot behind my shed. It's quite large, and the leaves remind me of lamb's ear. What is it?

Martha Giguere CORUNNA, MICHIGAN

Melinda: Some gardeners consider your plant, common mullein (*Verbascum thapsus*), a weed; others think it's a desirable flower. Originally brought here by colonists for its herbal properties, it has now spread throughout the United States and southern Canada, growing in disturbed sites, gardens, neglected areas and fields. The first year, mullein produces a rosette of fuzzy leaves, like those that appeared in your flowerpot. The second year, a tall flower stem emerges from the base, producing a spike of yellow blossoms. The parent plant then dies and the biennial cycle begins again with new seedlings the following year.

Q How do I control an abundance of grasshoppers in my garden?

Marge Berger NECEDAH, WISCONSIN

Melinda: Mobile grasshoppers are difficult to control. They lay their eggs in relatively dry, undisturbed sites and remain in this stage over winter. As they hatch, they move into gardens and fields where they feed on plants. Very dry winters and springs, as well as cold wet weather, reduce populations. But the insecticides labeled for the job also kill other insects, both beneficial and harmful ones. Semaspore bait is an organic control option. The active ingredient, *Nosema locustae*, is a naturally occurring single-cell protozoan that kills developing grasshoppers as well as mole, Mormon and field crickets. Apply around the garden you are trying to protect, following the instructions on the label, and sprinkle in and around the area for control. Young grasshoppers eat the bait and eventually die.

Q Is it normal for goldfinches to pluck the petals from black-eyed Susan flowers?

Allen Bodenschatz ST. LOUIS, MISSOURI

Kenn and Kimberly: Goldfinches are seed-eating birds and therein lies the answer to your interesting question. We have seen finches plucking petals from flowers in our yard as well. But they're not actually eating the petals. They're plucking the petals to get access to the tasty seeds. We've heard a few people express concern about the damage to their flowers, but we think the finches are just as beautiful as the flowers so it seems like a fair trade. We hope you agree!

Q How can I put less stress on my plants when I fertilize them?

Kathy Blakey SAINT PETERS, MISSOURI

Melinda: As a low-maintenance gardener, I prefer to use a low-nitrogen, slow-release fertilizer on my plants. It's a good choice because it releases small amounts of nutrients over a long period of time and also reduces the burn risk during hot, dry weather. I apply it once in spring, and then check the plants again in midsummer to see if they need a second application. If you garden in compost-amended or rich clay soils, you may only need one spring application for annuals. If you have a long growing season, sandy soil or a garden that's frequently irrigated, think about fertilizing twice. Soil tests are also helpful in determining what type of fertilizer you need, and when and how much to apply.

LITTLE JEWEL
Costa's, like this male, weigh in at only one-tenth of an ounce. Their crouched posture makes them look even smaller.

Q Two kinds of hummingbirds visit our yard: black-chinneds and Costa's. One is a young male Costa's whose throat patch is just beginning to show, and I always wonder how old he is. What is the life span of a hummingbird?

Terry Burkhart LANDERS, CALIFORNIA

Kenn and Kimberly: These tiny creatures don't live long. Based on banding studies, 7 or 8 years is a ripe old age for most hummingbirds in the wild. Ruby-throated hummingbirds have lived 9 years, and one banded female broad-tailed hummingbird in Colorado made it to 12. A zoo that's properly set up to care for these birds may stretch longevity: Two black-chinned hummingbirds at the Arizona-Sonora Desert Museum in Tucson lived to 13 or 14 years old. We don't have much information on the Costa's hummingbird, but a male with his gorget (throat patch) just developing would be a little less than 1 year old.

Q Is this hummingbird taking a nap? It landed on this branch after feeding, leaned back for about a minute and then took off!

Charles Hoysa WARRENTON, VIRGINIA

Kenn and Kimberly: You probably caught your visitor preening or in midstretch. With super long bills and tiny feet, hummingbirds strike pretty odd poses while preening their feathers. Hummingbirds also stretch, just like we do when we get up from the table after a meal. Sometimes they will pause in an odd pose and hold it for up to a minute, for no obvious reason.

Q Is there a way to keep woodpeckers from attacking wooden siding?

Robyn Long
GREENLAND, NEW HAMPSHIRE

Kenn and Kimberly: Discouraging woodpeckers is a challenge, but there are a few things you can try. Reflective streamers are the most effective, but any item that moves or flutters makes a good deterrent. Create these streamers yourself by cutting a mylar balloon or aluminum foil into thin strips, taping them to a small dowel rod, and attaching it to the top of any area that you want to protect from woodpeckers. Keep in mind that if the woodpeckers keep coming back to one spot, the wood may be infested with some kind of wood-boring insects.

Q Is June too late in the season to put out an oriole feeder?

Dominic LeRose LAKE BLUFF, ILLINOIS

Kenn and Kimberly: What a joy it is to tell you that Baltimore orioles should be in your area all summer. So, yes, we encourage you to set up a feeder. Keep in mind that while they visit feeders during spring migration and into early summer, orioles are very secretive during the nesting season. If they're nesting in your yard, the reward comes when they bring their young to your feeders. In addition to sugar-water feeders, try adding oranges cut in half. Many types of feeders designed for this purpose are now available, but simply impaling the orange halves on a stick or tree branch also works.

Q How do I keep yellow jackets out of my birdhouses?

Gai Murray WESTMINSTER, COLORADO

Kenn and Kimberly: Yellow jackets and other wasps chew up bits of wood to create paper, using it to fashion elaborate hanging nests. They're attracted to birdhouses, which offer sheltered nesting spots. Don't use pesticides on the birdhouse to keep wasps out—that's harmful for the birds, too. Instead, rub a bar of soap on the inside of the birdhouse roof. The slick surface makes it impossible for the wasps to attach the base of their nests to the roof, so they give up and go elsewhere.

Q After we brush our dog, we set the clean fur out for birds. Does the insulation help them in winter?

Jane Carter FALMOUTH, MASSACHUSETTS

Kenn and Kimberly: That's an imaginative way to recycle. Many birds use animal hair as nest lining material if it's available; for example, in the past, chipping sparrows were famous for using horsehair in their nests. Most birds only use their nests for raising young, and they don't sleep in those nests at other times of the year. However, bluebirds roost in boxes during the winter, and a well-insulated nest left over from summer might help on the coldest nights.

Q I discovered this newly made nest while prepping my fall garden. What bird nests this late in the year?

Anna Perea LOVELAND, COLORADO

Kenn and Kimberly: You're right, it's an uncommon time of year for nest-building, as well as an unusual location! In your area of Colorado, the builder is most likely a house sparrow. While these enterprising little birds usually place their nests inside holes in trees or structures, they'll sometimes put them in more open places like this spot on your tractor. They also build nests throughout the year. We can't be sure from the photo, but it's possible this nest wasn't made by a bird. It could be the work of some small mammal, maybe a mouse or one of the native wood rats.

Q I came across a group of these butterflies in October. Shouldn't they be heading south?

Susan Higbie GROSSE POINTE FARMS, MICHIGAN

Kenn and Kimberly: You are lucky to have witnessed a fascinating phenomenon—the migration of painted lady butterflies. They're not common in Michigan and the upper Midwest, but once every few years they suddenly show up in big numbers. This typically happens in summer or fall. The monarch butterflies that migrate through Michigan in autumn are headed south to the mountains of Mexico, but painted ladies don't have such a definite destination, and they may be migrating in any direction.

Q How did our dwarf Alberta spruce become so misshapen?

Peggy Ward CECIL, OHIO

Melinda: It is not unusual to see this type of growth on a dwarf Alberta spruce. The dwarf conifer originated from a mutation discovered on a white spruce. Plants were propagated from the unique, compact growth. A branch will occasionally revert back to the larger, more robust white spruce. Simply remove the larger branch at the bark collar, near the base of the growth. Do this as soon as possible to prevent it from ruining the shape of your spruce.

Q This bird hung out with a house finch at my sunflower seed feeder. It looks like a house finch, but the coloring is not typical. What kind of bird is this?

Jean Bullock DU QUOIN, ILLINOIS

Kenn and Kimberly: What you have there is a house finch with a fascinating color variation. Male house finches are usually marked with red, but sometimes those red areas are replaced with orange or yellow or some of both. The red pigment in the feathers is affected by what the finch eats, so there might have been deficiencies in the bird's diet back when this set of feathers was growing in. If this individual continues to visit your yard, you may see it develop the normal red coloring the next time it molts new feathers.

Q Is it safe to put out tinsel from my Christmas tree for the birds to use as nesting material?

Debbie Greenwaldt WAUKESHA, WISCONSIN

Kenn and Kimberly: We admire your interest in helping the birds. However, because unnatural materials like tinsel (and Easter grass) pose a potential strangling hazard, they are not safe nesting materials. Even yarn and string can be dangerous, especially if the strands are too long. Some wild bird feeding stores sell balls of nesting materials that are safe for birds, but providing nest material isn't really necessary. Birds are very good at finding natural materials on their own.

Q We see juncos only when the weather is cold or a cold front comes in. They don't stay around every day during the winter season. Where do they go?

Suzanne Nassar BROOKFIELD, CONNECTICUT

Kenn and Kimberly: Although juncos may stay in the same general area all winter, their daily activities often change with the weather. A junco flock may stay out in the woods and fields as long as the weather is mild, foraging for the seeds of grasses and weeds. When conditions turn harsh, especially if the ground is covered with snow or ice, those same juncos may move a considerable distance to backyards with well-stocked bird feeders. But they won't necessarily stay there after the next thaw arrives.

HOP TO IT
The next time a junco forages for food in your yard, pay attention to its stride, which is more of a hop than a walk. It stands out among flocks of finches or sparrows.

ATTRACT MORE CARDINALS

A tube or hopper feeder full of black oil sunflower seeds is the best way to lure these bold red birds to backyards across the eastern U.S. When they visit, take note of their territorial behaviors.

Q What causes a northern cardinal to raise or lower its crest?

Larry Thompson IRVING, TEXAS

Kenn and Kimberly: Northern cardinals raise or lower their crests at will. The position of the crest can be a signal to other cardinals, but the meaning of the signal seems to vary. When one male is aggressively driving another one away, it may flatten its crest completely, while the losing bird raises its crest high. When males are putting on courtship displays to woo females, they raise their crests in some displays and lower them in others. Their body language must be clear to other cardinals, but we human observers have to watch the rest of their behavior for more clues.

Q While hiking at Radnor Lake in Nashville last winter, we saw several bluebirds with variable coloring. Some had bright colors and others, muted hues. Were the differences due to the season or was it a mix of males and females?

Amy Vehec FRANKLIN, TENNESSEE

Kenn and Kimberly: That's a really good observation. Male and female eastern bluebirds look different—adult males wear brilliant blue and deep orange-brown, but females are also beautiful with their softer colors, blue-gray on the back and dull orange on the chest. The difference is obvious if you study a pair at their nest in summer. But in winter you can find even more variation, because young males aren't as richly hued as fully adult males, and young females are paler and grayer than adult females. It's fascinating to see the differences among individuals in a winter bluebird flock.

Q A large flock of vultures roosted in my cottonwood trees last winter. The ground was solid white and the smell was not pleasant. Is roosting a seasonal event? If not, can I encourage them to roost elsewhere?

Ginger Ferguson WEATHERFORD, TEXAS

Kenn and Kimberly: After a day of working as nature's cleanup crew, vultures gather at night in communal roosts. Unfortunately, once they find a good roosting site, they may return year after year. It's illegal to use lethal methods on vultures, but it may be possible to scare them away. Try disturbing them with loud noises or squirting a water hose when they try to settle in for the evening, and they may seek another site. If they're not so easily discouraged, you might hire a professional animal-control company, but make sure they have a reputation for operating legally and not harming the birds.

Turkey vulture

Q Every winter I grow herbs in an east-facing bay window. I start rosemary, oregano, basil and cilantro outside at the end of summer, then transplant and bring them in the house, but they never survive. What's the best way to grow herbs indoors?

Marge Berger NECEDAH, WISCONSIN

Melinda: Monitor the growing conditions in your window. Light is usually a limiting factor when growing herbs indoors during the winter, especially in Northern locations. Make sure nearby trees, neighboring houses or other structures are not limiting the sunlight reaching the plants. Add artificial lights to solve this problem. Next, monitor the day and night temperature in this area. The thickness of the window glass in your current growing space may be causing temperature fluctuations. Look for another space that is free of drafts with more suitable day and night temperatures if there's a concern. And last, consider purchasing plants from a greenhouse or starting from seeds indoors. The transition indoors may be putting too much stress on your plants.

Q My crocosmia never blooms; it just produces green leaves. I've tried fertilizing and moving some plants to new spots. What's going on?

Donnie Woods RIDGECREST, CALIFORNIA

Melinda: Shade, excessive fertilizer and overcrowding often prevent crocosmia from flowering. Make sure your plants are receiving at least six, preferably eight or more, hours of sunlight each day. Avoid high-nitrogen fertilizers that encourage lots of leaf growth and discourage flowering. Sometimes excessive growth leads to overcrowding, which also discourages flowering. Dig and divide overcrowded plants if needed.

MEET THE EXPERTS

Kenn and Kimberly Kaufman are the duo behind the Kaufman Field Guide series. They speak and lead bird trips all over the world.

Melinda Myers is a nationally known, award-winning garden expert, TV/radio host and author of more than 20 books.

Grow for Your Zone

Find the number associated with your region, and then stick to plants that will thrive in your area.

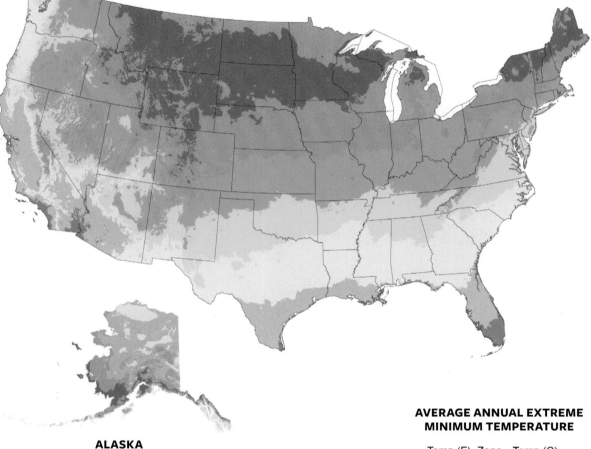

ALASKA

HAWAII

USDA PLANT HARDINESS ZONES

Hardiness zones reflect the average annual minimum cold temperatures for an area. If it's difficult to precisely locate your city on the map here, use the interactive version on the USDA's website, *planthardiness.ars.usda.gov*. Enter your ZIP code, and your hardiness zone and average minimum winter temperature range will appear.

AVERAGE ANNUAL EXTREME MINIMUM TEMPERATURE

Temp (F)	Zone	Temp (C)
-60 to -50	1	-51.1 to -45.6
-50 to -40	2	-45.6 to -40
-40 to -30	3	-40 to -34.4
-30 to -20	4	-34.4 to -28.9
-20 to -10	5	-28.9 to -23.3
-10 to 0	6	-23.3 to -17.8
0 to 10	7	-17.8 to -12.2
10 to 20	8	-12.2 to -6.7
20 to 30	9	-6.7 to -1.1
30 to 40	10	-1.1 to 4.4
40 to 50	11	4.4 to 10
50 to 60	12	10 to 15.6
60 to 70	13	15.6 to 21.1

Birdhouse Guidelines

Discover which dwellings are best for your backyard birds.

SPECIES	DIMENSIONS	HOLE	PLACEMENT	COLOR	NOTES
Eastern bluebird	5x5x8" h.	1½" centered 6" above floor	5-10' high in the open; sunny area	light earth tones	likes open areas, especially facing a field
Tree swallow	5x5x6" h.	1" centered 4" above floor	5-8' high in the open; 50-100% sun	light earth tones or gray	within 2 miles of pond or lake
Purple martin	multiple apts. 6x6x6" ea.	2⅛" centered 2¼" above floor	15-20' high in the open	white	open yard without tall trees; near water
Tufted titmouse	4x4x8" h.	1¼"	4-10' high	light earth tones	prefers to live in or near woods
Chickadee	4x4x8" h. or 5x5" base	1⅛" centered 6" above floor	4-8' high	light earth tones	small tree thicket
Nuthatch	4x4x10" h.	1¼" centered 7½" above floor	12-25' high on tree trunk	bark-covered or natural	prefers to live in or near woods
House wren	4x4x8" h. or 4x6" base	1" centered 6" above floor	5-10' high on post or hung in tree	light earth tones or white	prefers lower branches of backyard trees
Northern flicker	7x7x18" h.	2½" centered 14" above floor	8-20' high	light earth tones	put 4" of sawdust inside for nesting
Downy woodpecker	4x4x10" h.	1¼" centered 7½" above floor	12-25' high on tree trunk	simulate natural cavity	prefers own excavation; provide sawdust
Red-headed woodpecker	6x6x15" h.	2" centered 6-8" above floor	8-20' high on post or tree trunk	simulate natural cavity	needs sawdust for nesting
Wood duck	10x10x24" h.	4x3" elliptical 20" above floor	2-5' high on post over water, or 12-40' high on tree facing water	light earth tones or natural	needs 3-4" of sawdust or shavings for nesting
American kestrel	10x10x24" h.	4x3" elliptical 20" above floor	12-40' high on post or tree trunk	light earth tones or natural	needs open approach on edge of woodlot or in isolated tree
Screech-owl	10x10x24" h.	4x3" elliptical 20" above floor	2-5' high on post over water, or 12-40' high on tree	light earth tones or natural	prefers open woods or edge of woodlot

Note: With the exception of wrens and purple martins, birds do not tolerate swaying birdhouses. Birdhouses should be firmly anchored to a post, a tree or the side of a building.

Source: *Garden Birds of America* by George H. Harrison. Willow Creek Press, 1996.

Nest Boxes to Know

Welcome more bird families to your backyard with a variety
of cozy places for them to raise their young.

SONGBIRD HOUSE

Chickadees, titmice, bluebirds and wrens are the most
common backyard cavity nesters. They take up residence
in classic wood birdhouses, but they're very particular
about the size of the entrance hole. These songbirds
are most likely to raise a family in a box if the hole is
1 to 1½ inches in diameter.

WOODPECKER HOUSE

Entice woodpeckers
with boxes attached to
tree trunks, from 8 to
25 feet high. Add 4 inches
of wood shavings to the
floor for woodpeckers
to use as nesting material.
The preferred entrance
hole size varies by species.
Downies like 1¼ inches;
flickers favor 2½ inches.

SCREECH-OWL HOUSE

Hang a birdhouse for
screech-owls to nest in
the summer and roost
in winter. They will use
a box with an elliptical
entrance hole 4 inches
wide by 3 inches high.
Watch them peek their
heads out around dusk.
Bonus! Wood ducks are
attracted to the same
type of birdhouse.

PURPLE MARTIN HOUSE

Purple martins nest in colonies, so consider a six- to
12-cavity house. Being a martin landlord takes some
commitment, though. First set up the large multiunit
house 15 to 20 feet above ground—and then keep the
cavities clear of nonnative house sparrows.

BUY OR BUILD

Find birdhouses at your local big-box store or look for a pattern online and make your own.

Birds and Their Favorite Foods

	Nyjer (thistle) seed	Cracked corn	White proso millet	Black oil sunflower seed	Hulled sunflower seed	Beef suet	Fruit	Sugar water (nectar)*
Rose-breasted grosbeak				•	•			
Black-headed grosbeak				•	•			
Evening grosbeak		•	•	•	•			
Northern cardinal		•	•	•	•		•	
Indigo bunting	•				•			
Eastern towhee	•	•	•	•	•			
Dark-eyed junco	•	•	•	•	•			
White-crowned sparrow	•	•	•	•	•			
White-throated sparrow	•	•	•	•	•			
American tree sparrow	•	•	•		•			
Chipping sparrow	•	•	•		•			
Song sparrow	•	•	•		•			
House sparrow	•	•	•		•			
House finch	•	•	•	•	•			
Purple finch	•	•	•	•	•			
American goldfinch	•	•	•	•	•			
Pine siskin	•	•	•	•	•			
Scarlet tanager							•	•
Western tanager							•	•
Baltimore oriole							•	•
Red-winged blackbird		•		•	•			
Eastern bluebird							•	
Wood thrush							•	
American robin							•	
Gray catbird							•	
Northern mockingbird							•	
Brown thrasher							•	
Ruby-throated hummingbird								•
Anna's hummingbird								•
Broad-tailed hummingbird								•
Tufted titmouse	•			•	•	•		
Black-capped chickadee	•			•	•	•		
White-breasted nuthatch				•	•	•		
Carolina wren						•		
Cedar waxwing							•	
Woodpecker				•	•	•	•	
Scrub-jay		•		•	•	•	•	
Blue jay		•		•	•	•	•	
Mourning dove	•	•	•		•			
Northern bobwhite		•	•		•			
Ring-necked pheasant		•	•		•			
Canada goose		•						
Mallard		•						

* To make sugar water, mix 4 parts water with 1 part sugar. Boil, cool and serve. Store leftovers in the refrigerator for up to a week. Change feeder nectar every three to five days.

Source: *Garden Birds of America* by George H. Harrison. Willow Creek Press, 1996.

Choose a Seed Feeder

Find an option that attracts the birds you want to spot in your backyard.

HOPPER

This classic feeder is often in the shape of a house or barn and holds enough seed to feed birds for days. Hoppers are a surefire way to offer black oil sunflower seeds to finches, jays, cardinals, buntings and other perching birds. Many have suet cages on two sides, making them all-purpose feeders for every season.

TUBE

Tube feeders are available with small ports for thistle seed or larger ports for sunflower, safflower and mixed seed. If you want to attract small, clinging birds such as chickadees, titmice and finches, look for a tube feeder with small perches under the ports. The perches discourage bully birds and squirrels.

THISTLE

Designed to hold tiny thistle seeds (also sold as Nyjer), thistle feeders are a major draw for goldfinches. Feeders range from simple hanging mesh bags to plastic or metal tubes. You can even get ones that are a few feet long to feed an entire flock of finches or redpolls. Look for a thistle feeder that's easy to clean, as the small seeds can collect mold in enclosed tubes.

PLATFORM

These feeders hang from a tree branch or sit atop legs on the ground, and are always completely open. This gives large birds enough space to land and eat. Sparrows, jays, juncos and blackbirds visit platform feeders, but so do squirrels.

Find feeders like these, and more, at a big-box store, garden center or specialty bird store, or online.

Red-headed woodpeckers were my dad's favorite birds, so they will always have a special place in my heart. They fly through northwestern Indiana but don't stay long. I quietly snuck around to get a clear view of this one, but it flew off after only two photos. I was disappointed until I saw how great this shot turned out.

Paul Lawson NEW CARLISLE, INDIANA

Birds&Blooms